W9-ABA-140

HEROES AND LEGENDS

ROBIN HOOD

BY NEIL SMITH

ILLUSTRATED BY PETER DENNIS

ROSEN
PUBLISHING

New York

Published in 2015 by The Rosen Publishing Group, Inc.
29 East 21st Street, New York, NY 10010

First Edition

Library of Congress Cataloging-in-Publication Data

Smith, Neil (Historian)
Robin Hood/Neil Smith.
     pages cm. — (Heroes and legends)
Includes bibliographical references and index.
Originally published: Oxford : Osprey Publishing, 2014.
ISBN 978-1-4777-8139-5 (library bound)
1. Robin Hood (Legendary character—Juvenile literature. 2. Folklore and history—England—Juvenile literature. 3. Outlaws—England—Juvenile literature. I. Title.
PZ8.1.S6546R63 2015
398.22—dc23
                                                                            2014020517

CONTENTS

INTRODUCTION

Of all the myriad characters inhabiting England's vibrant past, two men stand out as representing something essential in the English identity. The first is King Arthur, who pulled the nation together in a common defense against invaders; the second is Robin Hood, who defied the odds to stand up to hypocrisy and injustice. Neither man may actually have existed, but they live on in the collective imagination, through the legends and myths told about them. This book focuses on Robin Hood, who remains as elusive today as he apparently did to the Sheriff of Nottingham during England's Middle Ages.

There are few in the English-speaking world that have never heard of Robin Hood. His name is synonymous with an outlaw whose motive is to do good deeds using unlawful methods. He is a trickster, fighter, lover, adventurer; he looks like Errol Flynn, or Russell Crowe, or Kevin Costner, or any of his television incarnations; he wears Lincoln green, carries a longbow, and knows how to use it. He lives deep in Sherwood Forest, leads a band of colorful outlaws known as the Merry Men, and his passion is reserved for the always-beautiful Maid Marian. Robin Hood takes from the rich and gives to the poor, and he fights against the corruption of the local law and the established Church. He is a placeholder for better times when Royal authority is more judiciously applied. All of the above is a combination of myth, fabrication, and pure fiction – almost all of it anyway.

We know about a man called Robin Hood because people first told stories or sung ballads about an outlaw now lost to the historical record and then wrote them down. As time passed, later interpretations entered the tales as contemporary motifs, and the exploits of other bandits were used to freshen up the stories for new audiences. The legend of Robin Hood coalesced through that process. The core of the legend is contained in a few collected ballads under the title of *A Gest of Robyn Hode*, and dated to around 1450, before the English Reformation. While it is a bit too convenient, it is reasonable to argue that the stories originating after the Reformation of the 16th century form the myth of Robin Hood. From after the mid-1500s, new characters are introduced, including some merely for entertainment value, and new stories emerge. The greatest change, though, is that of Robin Hood himself. His status changes from yeoman to disaffected nobleman; he has a love-interest where none existed before; and he becomes less brutal. This is also where the notion of Robin taking from the rich to give to the poor enters the story, along with the idea that Robin was fighting oppression while awaiting the arrival of the true king. The myth reaches its apotheosis in the Technicolor delights of *The Adventures of Robin Hood*, with Errol Flynn dressed in the Lincoln green, but the seemingly timeless story of Robin Hood has endured for new generations and audiences and will no doubt continue to do so.

Robin Hood and the bishop. (Bridgeman)

THE LEGEND OF ROBIN HOOD

We do not know the exact origins of the Robin Hood legend, but we do know the means by which it was disseminated. The first stories were ballads passed along by itinerant singers who visited fairs and public gatherings to entertain the public. A canon of songs soon sprang up, with little embellishments no doubt added here and there to suit individual styles and target audiences. Robin's popularity spread so far that by the 15th century monks were taking note of the ballads and writing them down. Later in that century, around the 1490s, the ballads appeared in print for the first time. The bulk of the stories that make up the legend were collected under the title *A Gest of Robyn Hode*, a 456-line poem divided into eight "fyttes." A couple of stories found in the 18th century Percy Folio manuscript, from which much of the Robin Hood myth stems, may also be traced back to the legend and are included here.

Robin Hood and the Knight

Barnesdale Forest, teeming with game and deer, was Robin Hood's sanctuary as well as his home in those days, and free from interference from the law.

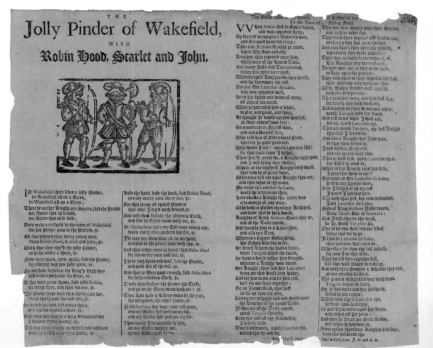

A page from *The Jolly Pinder of Wakefield*, a ballad first published in 1632, which includes the account of Robin Hood and Little John's first meeting.

The forest extended for many miles across south Yorkshire and down into Nottinghamshire, where it joined with Sherwood Forest. An army of a thousand men could hide in those woods with impunity, though Robin's band of Merry Men probably numbered closer to one hundred. One day, as Robin was leaning against a tree deep in the forest, three of his men approached. His trusted lieutenant, Little John, was there, along with William Scarlett, and the diminutive Much the Miller's Son. Robin decided that he wanted to entertain a "guest" for dinner; some high-ranking noble would do nicely, and ideally a baron or a knight. He told his three companions what he wanted, but warned that they should not pick on farmers or yeomen. Also, Robin added, those knights or squires who were known to be good people should be left in peace. Archbishops and priests, on the other hand, were fair game, and the Sheriff of Nottingham was on the top of the list of potential victims.

As the sun sank slowly towards the horizon, Robin instructed Little John to take Scarlett and Much and to go to Sayles Farm, near the old Roman road called Watling Street, where they were sure to find a suitable target.

When Little John and his companions arrived at Sayles Farm, they took up positions along the road, with their bows strung and ready for action. They looked up and down the road, but no one appeared from either direction for long hours. Then, suddenly, away from the road, they saw a mounted figure making his way through the woods, along a concealed track. The traveller was a knight, but not one that would fit the beautiful chivalric images carefully drawn by monks in illuminated manuscripts. This dreary-looking knight sagged in his saddle, one foot in the stirrup while the other swung loose. The rider's hood drooped over his eyes, and he was as sorry a sight as the bandits had ever seen. The knight's pitiful condition, however, did not stop them from stepping out of the trees into his path. With his arrow nocked, John extended Robin's invitation to dinner.

"I had intended to eat in Doncaster or Blyth," the startled knight replied, "but I bear no personal malice towards Robin Hood, so I will go with you." He bade Little John to lead the way.

When the little group returned to Robin's lodge, the knight introduced himself, "Sir Richard of the Lea, at your service," while the outlaws prepared a sumptuous dinner of bread, wine, deer, and wildfowl. The knight was thoroughly impressed with both his reception and his meal, and promised to return the honor if he ever came back this way. Robin appreciated the appreciation, but remarked that it was unusual that he, a mere yeoman, should be entertaining a man of such high status in this way. It was obvious from Robin's tone that Sir Richard was expected to pay at least his fair share for the food. The knight, however, said apologetically that he had no money to offer for such a feast, not any more than ten shillings. Robin turned to Little John and asked him to check Sir Richard's belongings, adding that he would take anything and everything above that amount, though he would

In 1883, author and illustrator Howard Pyle published *The Merry Adventures of Robin Hood of Great Renown in Nottinghamshire*. This book reworked the old ballads and presented them in a modern, cohesive form, while emphasizing Robin's status as a hero who robbed from the rich to give to the poor. While the writing style is now dated, the book remains one of the most influential works about the outlaw. Many of the illustrations that Pyle drew for the book are reprinted in this one. Here, Robin stops the sorrowful knight. The overly ornate decorations betray the highly romantic Victorian style adopted by Pyle in his book.

lend the knight some money if he really needed more. The outlaws and their guest didn't have long to wait before Little John returned, confirming Sir Richard's poverty.

Surprised, Robin was also curious about how his guest had been reduced to his current situation. He asked if Sir Richard had been raised to his knightly status from the yeoman class due to some battlefield distinction, or if he had behaved immorally, and so been reduced in his station as a punishment. The knight denied both, confirming that his nobility was hereditary, but he told Robin that, over the last two years, he had been forced to raise 400 pounds to save his son from a false charge of murder. He had been forced to borrow so heavily from the Abbot of St. Mary's Abbey that if he could not repay the debt he would be landless and forced to leave England.

"Have you no friends to help you?" Robin asked.

Sir Richard replied, "Those I thought were my friends scattered when my misfortune became clear."

Robin considered this and then had Little John bring him 400 pounds from the outlaws' treasury. Little John, for his part, pointed out how threadbare the knight's clothes were and how he clearly needed new livery to truly dress to his status.

Robin said, "You'll make a fine tailor," to which Little John quickly measured both the knight and some suitable cloth with his longbow, much to the amusement of Will Scarlett. John was indeed a handy tailor, and he soon produced brand new livery for the knight. To complete the man's transformation: Will Scarlett gave him a new pair of boots; Little John handed over a pair of shiny spurs; and Robin led out a gray horse for the man to ride. Sir Richard was grateful beyond words for his new wardrobe, but the generous Robin was not finished.

"No self-respecting knight could travel without a squire," he pointed out. "I'm sure John would be happy to oblige."

Little John nodded his agreement. Then all that was left to do was conclude their bargain, whereby the knight would pay off the Abbot at once, and then repay his debt to Robin within 12 months.

Dressed in his new finery and mounted astride his new horse, Sir Richard left the outlaws with renewed confidence and hope. Little John gathered what he needed for the journey and strode out alongside his temporary new "master." Robin and his Merry Men watched them go, satisfied that they had made a new friend and ally.

Robin Hood and the Potter

When Spring turned to Summer in the forest, the woods burst into life with birds singing happily in the trees, surrounded by fresh blossoms, while Robin Hood and his Merry Men held their councils in the sunshine. Though such mornings seemed idyllic, these men were still outlaws and stayed alert in case the Sheriff's men might creep up on them. Therefore, when one of the Merry Men spotted a horse and cart approaching across open ground nearby, he immediately brought the cart-driver to the attention of Robin. Robin recognized the visitor as a potter who often travelled that way to avoid paying the penny road-toll. Little John also recognized the potter.

"He's a stubborn one, that potter, but a good fighter," he told the Merry Men. "I once fought the man in nearby Wentbridge, and I can still feel his knuckles." Mischievously, Little John declared, "I'll wager 40 shillings that no man among us could force that potter to pay to pass this way." Robin Hood could not resist the challenge.

The Merry Men took cover in the trees and undergrowth and waited until the potter came closer. Robin jumped out in front of the cart, grabbed the reins of the potter's horse, and told him to stop. The potter asked what Robin wanted, to which Robin replied that the potter had "oft passed this way through my forest, but had never paid a toll."

Indignantly, the potter asked for the outlaw's name, but if he recognized the words "Robin Hood" he did not show it, and seemed unimpressed by the answer.

He told Robin, "I will pay nothing to receive permission to go through an illegal roadblock. Now let go of my horse, or it'll be the worse for you." Robin did not let go of the reins, so the potter dismounted, went back to his cart, and pulled out a two-handed staff. He repeated his threat that Robin would be in trouble now. Robin dropped the reins and drew his sword.

The amused Merry Men gathered round as Robin picked up his small buckler shield, and the two men squared off ready to fight.

The potter struck first, knocking the buckler out of Robin Hood's hand. Robin ducked to retrieve the shield, but then the potter hit him across the neck, and the outlaw fell to the ground. The shocked Merry Men rushed in to assist their leader. The situation suddenly looked very bleak for the potter, who found himself in the midst of a heavily armed crowd of outlaws. He complained that they had been very rude to prevent a man from travelling.

Even as he helped Robin to his feet, Little John's interest lay in who had won their wager. Reluctantly, Robin was forced to acknowledge that he had

Robin Hood greets the potter.
Artwork by Peter Dennis.

lost, and so owed Little John the money. Robin also conceded the potter's point regarding his delay, and, rather than kill the man, offered his friendship.

Robin then saw an opportunity for a bit of mischief. He asked if the potter would be willing to exchange clothing so that Robin could go safely into Nottingham on the pretense of selling the pots, while the potter waited in the forest. Although suspicious, the potter thought it best to agree with the outlaw chief, and the two switched outfits. Little John reminded Robin that the Sheriff of Nottingham was neither a friend nor a stupid enemy, and that it was a dangerous game he intended to play. Robin laughed and waved away his friend's concerns. He then took the potter's horse and cart and set out alone for Nottingham.

It was not long before Robin reached the gates of Nottingham. The guards waved him through without comment, and he stabled his horse before setting up his stall next to the Sheriff's gate in the marketplace. Once he had laid out his wares, Robin called out for buyers who might appreciate the cheapest prices for quality pots. Customers soon descended on Robin, realizing that he was underselling the pots, and hoping to take advantage of this obviously naïve potter. The buying frenzy continued until Robin had only five pots left, and those he sent to the Sheriff's wife for free. She was delighted at the surprise gift and came out to thank the potter in person. She also promised to buy more of his pots the next time he was selling in town and then invited him to dine with the Sheriff and herself.

Robin followed the Sheriff's wife back to her house, but, on entering, he immediately came face to face with the Sheriff standing in the hall. The Sheriff didn't show any sign of recognizing Robin, but instead seemed curious about his wife's unexpected guest. When she explained about the potter's generosity with his wares, the Sheriff said he was most welcome to dine with them and led the way to the table.

As they sat down to eat, two of the Sheriff's men, standing near the table, began discussing a wager of 40 shillings on who was the best archer between them. Robin's ears pricked up, but, as yet, he said nothing. When the meal was over, the Sheriff and Robin made their way to the archery range to watch the contest. Robin saw that the Sheriff's men were obviously novices and shot their arrows too quickly. He turned to the Sheriff and suggested that, if he had a bow, then everyone would witness a better shot than they had seen so far.

The Sheriff quickly ordered a bow brought for the potter. Robin strung the bow, but, as he made ready to shoot, found himself unimpressed by the quality of the weapon. Nevertheless, his first shot missed the target peg by less than 12 inches. Robin's second shot, however, shattered the peg, easily winning the contest against the now-shamed Sheriff's men.

The Sheriff, unlike his men, was greatly amused, and asked this potter if he would like to have his own new bow – one that, he claimed, had previously belonged to Robin Hood. The Sheriff asked the potter if he knew of Robin Hood, and naturally Robin denied knowing any such person. The Sheriff said that Robin was a notorious local outlaw and promised that if the potter came

WEAPONS OF AN OUTLAW

If we believe the myth and legend of Robin Hood, it is hard to imagine a more successful outlaw. As far as we know, Robin Hood spent almost his entire adult life living in a particular area in England, where he led a band of fiercely loyal retainers, and eluded every attempt to capture him. Like any professional, however, Robin Hood had to be highly proficient with the tools of his trade, which in his case were the bow, sword, and quarterstaff.

It is difficult to picture Robin Hood without his longbow. Indeed, he was the consummate archer, whose incredible accuracy would make a legendary figure even without all of his other attributes. He must also have possessed great strength because the bow was not a simple weapon to use, despite its appearance.

Robin's bow would have stood at least as tall as himself at around six and a half feet in length. It would have been a self-bow, meaning it was made from one piece of wood, probably fashioned from a Yew or Ash tree. An English yeoman would typically lean into his bow, pushing forward with his left arm while holding the hemp or flax string taught with the fingers of his right hand. That would require anywhere between 50–60 pounds-force for hunting, or 100–180 pounds-force, or 440–800 Newtons, to draw the bow into its full kite-shape when ready to shoot. The length of the draw would equal the length of the arrow,

around three feet. Then, Robin would hold his position in complete stillness while he sighted his target down the shaft of the arrow. A typical trained archer might expect to easily hit his target at 150 yards, but one of Robin's ability would certainly have fancied his chances at ranges of up to 350 yards. Any living target in between those distances could not expect to survive the encounter even if human and wearing armor. Moreover, in the unlikely event that Robin missed his target, the average rate of shooting for longbowmen was an impressive six shots per minute, and there is no record of Robin Hood missing twice.

The longbow was Robin's main weapon, but it was only useful at a distance. When it came to close combat, Robin would have drawn his sword. Given that he carried a bow, it is unlikely that Robin carried anything larger than the one-handed sword that was common for fighting men in the Medieval period. This was a straight, double-edged steel weapon, measuring around three feet in length, with a crossbar separating the blade from the grip, or hilt, and a metal ball, the pommel, on the end of the handle to add weight to the

An English longbowman from the first half of the 14th century. It is soldiers like these that have often served as the basis for depictions of Robin Hood. (Artwork by Gerry Embleton from Osprey Publishing's WAR 11: *English Longbowman 1330-1515*)

back of the sword. The counterweight at the rear gave the sword a balance point close to the hilt, and made it easier to work with in combat. There was little need for finesse with this sword as there would be little time in the heat of the fight for anything more than lusty cutting and thrusting.

In addition, Robin Hood carried a buckler. This was a small, convex shield held easily in one hand or fastened to the forearm and designed to deflect blows. However, the skilled fighter could use the buckler as an offensive weapon, either to punch his opponent or to hook an arm or sword.

Rounding off the well-armed outlaw's close-range weapons was the dagger. This was a ubiquitous piece of equipment for almost any man in the period. Daggers were shorter than swords, though often designed the same way, with a double-edged blade connecting to a suitable handgrip. The common method for using a dagger was to thrust with its extremely sharp point, which could pierce the joints in armor, rather than to slash, which could be easily deflected.

The other personal combat weapon used by Robin Hood and his Merry Men was the staff, sometimes called the quarterstaff, though that term was not used in the period. It is, perhaps, the weapon most often associated with the legendary outlaws. This staff was about seven or eight feet long, made from hardwood, and thin enough for a man to grasp tightly but thick enough not to bend or break easily. Many staves were little more than sturdy branches, stripped of leaves and twigs for the purpose. The staff was too large for single-handed use, and some have argued that it took the name quarterstaff after the way it was held about a quarter of the way along the shaft. The main method of fighting with the staff was to block and parry the opponent's blows while seeking an opening to thrust the shaft horizontally into his softer regions. A blow with a shaft was unlikely to kill, and it was therefore often used as a training aid in learning to fight.

Nevertheless, with so much material readily available in the forest, Robin Hood's men would find a staff quick and cheap to procure. Of all his weapons, Robin appears to have been least proficient with his staff, famously losing his fight to Little John on their first encounter at the log bridge and receiving a quick bath in the stream for his troubles.

with the Sheriff's men on a foray into the woods the next day, he would be guaranteed to meet the outlaw.

Robin prepared the potter's horse and cart for the ride into the forest early the next morning. He said goodbye to the Sheriff's wife and gave her a gold ring in appreciation of her hospitality. She thanked Robin and watched as her husband and his men made their way out of the town and into the woods.

Once the town was out of sight and the Sheriff's party rode among the trees, approaching the area where Robin had left his Merry Men the previous day, Robin took out a horn and blew it loudly. In a matter of moments, several score of Merry Men, including Little John, swarmed out from the undergrowth in which they had been hiding and surrounded the Sheriff's party, holding them at sword- and arrow-point.

Robin jumped down from the cart as Little John asked him how he had got on while standing in for the potter. Robin pointed to the stunned Sheriff and said that he had brought him back as a reward for all his hard work. Little John was greatly amused and exclaimed that the Sheriff would probably give 100 pounds never to have seen Robin Hood. That sounded fair to Robin, who turned to the dismayed Sheriff and told him that he would be allowed to return to Nottingham, but that he would do so without his horse and gear. Indeed, he would not be returning to Nottingham at all if it were not for the generosity of his good wife.

That night, when the Sheriff arrived back home, his wife asked him how he had fared in the forest, and if he had brought Robin Hood back with him.

The Sheriff cursed Robin, shouting, "Damn him, and the Devil take him!" He told her what had happened and said that the only thing he had left from his trip to the forest was a white horse, given to him by the outlaw – and that that was a present for her.

The Sheriff's wife burst out laughing. "Robin Hood," she said, "has taken the proper price of his pots, and left us with a story to tell."

Back in the forest, Robin asked the potter how much his pots were actually worth. The potter lamented that he was down by two Nobles through not going to Nottingham. Robin promised him ten pounds as compensation, and that he would always be considered a friend when he passed through the forest, tolls or not. The two men then parted company as friends.

The Knight Pays His Debt

The Abbot of St. Mary's had gathered his advisors, in order to remind them that a visiting knight was due to pay his debt that day. He anticipated the knight's failure to pay with some relish, but his Prior chided the Abbot for being so flippant about another man's misfortune. They were then joined by the corpulent High Cellarer, who said he had come to collect the Abbot. They were due to go and meet the knight at the court of the High Justice of England. Like the Abbot, the Cellarer was full of cheer at the expected windfall, because he also believed the knight would not turn up and that his land would therefore be forfeit. Much to the surprise and chagrin of the Cellarer and Abbot, he did.

Sir Richard of the Lea had come accompanied, as was proper for a knight in those days, by a squire and servants. On their approach to the court, the knight ordered these men to disguise themselves with weeds, to give the impression of having travelled by sea. The porter welcomed them at the gatehouse, but was surprised to see that such poorly dressed men had such a fine horse in tow. Sir Richard therefore ordered his horse stabled before meeting with the Abbot, so that the animal did not betray the effect of their disguise.

When he entered the Abbot's Hall, the knight knelt in homage. The Abbot didn't ask him to stand, but asked immediately for his money. Sir Richard claimed poverty, and so the Abbot asked, "Why have you bothered to come at all, if you cannot or will not pay?"

"To plead for more time," the knight replied. He then turned to the Justice and asked him for help with his predicament, but the Justice shook his head, siding with the Abbot. The Abbot then rejected his debtor's pleas.

"You are no true knight," he added, "but a false knight!" and the Abbot dismissed the knight, insisting that he should leave their presence immediately. The Justice then turned to the Abbot, barely concealing his amusement, and asked how much money he would give the knight to hurry him off his land. "One hundred pounds?" the Abbot suggested, but the Justice thought that was not enough. "Give him 200," he ordered the Abbot.

Sir Richard finally stood up, tired of this level of discourtesy towards a man of his rank. He proclaimed, "Keep your purses closed. There is no amount of money in England that would force me to part with my lands." Before the two men could react, he walked over to a nearby table and threw down 400 pounds from his bag. The Abbot stared open-mouthed, realizing his chance to grab the knight's estates so cheaply had been lost.

Having so dramatically paid his debt, Sir Richard promptly walked out without so much as a backward glance. He retrieved his horse and changed out of his "poor" clothes, before returning home to Uttersdale where his Lady waited anxiously. He told her how they were now free of the Abbot's debt, and they had Robin Hood to thank for it.

A statue of Robin Hood in Sherwood Forest. (Hemis / Alamy)

Though he intended to waste no time, it would be a while longer before Sir Richard could repay his debt to Robin Hood. When he had accrued the 400 pounds he needed, the knight sent word to Robin that he was ready. He mustered a company of 100 archers, supplied them with bows and sheaves of arrows, and dressed them in his red and white livery. He then marched his new retinue out in the direction of Barnesdale. They had not travelled far when they came upon a crowd of villagers blocking a bridge over which the men needed to cross. Riding forward, Sir Richard ascertained that the villagers were threatening a young man who had defeated the local champion in a wrestling match.

Driven forward by a sense of justice, the knight pushed his horse through the crowd while his archers followed with their arrows nocked. The crowd pulled back from this threat, allowing the young man to escape. Seeing that this had inflamed the anger of the crowd rather than dissipating it, Sir Richard ordered his men to bring wine for the villagers. As he expected, this relaxed the villagers, dispelling their anger. The young man had been saved, and the crowd were happy, but Sir Richard's scheduled meeting with Robin had been seriously delayed.

RICHARD OF THE LEA COMES TO ROBIN'S CAMP (PREVIOUS PAGE)

I first encountered Robin Hood in literature, as opposed to seeing Richard Greene in tights on the TV, in the wonderful Howard Pyle edition of the tales, illustrated and written by him in a rich pastiche of the high Gothic popular in the late Victorian period. His description of a fantasy medieval England in which even my own workaday market town, once in the center of Sherwood, becomes "Fair Mansfield" and sprouts turrets and walls, is quite enchanting. Although my own taste in maturity is for the darker Robin of the ballads, I decided to take Pyle's careful and highly colored reworking of the stories as the basis of my series of paintings. Not only did Pyle invent the Caribbean pirate, as we know the type today, but he put his stamp firmly on the image of Robin and his Merry Men.

In the long tale called *The Gest of Robin Hood* part of the story concerns Robin's encounter on the road with a knight fallen on hard times called Sir Richard of the Lea who has a castle not far from Nottingham. It may have been at modern Annesley - "Anne's Lea."

Sir Richard's plight is a complex one. Basically, he has become entangled with the corrupt and avaricious clergy at an abbey who are demanding repayment of a debt, and who will take his castle and lands if he can't pay. This was a common ploy of the ever-growing and powerful monasteries in medieval England.

When Robin brings the tattered and impecunious knight into his camp, he finds that Little John has brought in a Bishop and his entourage who have a treasure chest and much other rich booty. The strongbox is opened with a two-handed sword, according to Howard Pyle, to reveal hundreds of gold pieces. With this Robin is able to help the knight out of his difficulty.

This illustration contains a "group shot" of some of the better known characters in the band, including Maid Marion, perhaps the least convincing of the outlaws, who doesn't appear in the ballads and was created in Tudor times, maybe to add a leavening of romance to what had become rather coarse and raucous performances of rustic Robin Hood plays.

- Peter Dennis

Robin Hood and the High Cellarer

In the forest, although it was the agreed day for Sir Richard to repay his debt to Robin Hood, the outlaw was in no mood to celebrate, because the knight had not yet turned up. Little John reassured Robin that, "The sun has not yet gone down, and I am sure that a knight such as Sir Richard can be trusted to honour his obligation before the day is over." Robin did not want to hear any excuses, so he ordered Little John to take Much and Scarlett up to the Sayles Farm and find him another "guest;" perhaps a messenger, someone who could tell good jokes, or even a poor man that might need their help.

The three men strapped on their weapons and picked up their bows, before making their way through the woods to the farm where they had first met Sir Richard. Once there, they took up positions on both sides of the road and settled down to wait. It was not long before Little John noticed a Benedictine monk slowly approaching on a horse with a retinue of over 50 armed men around him. Little John turned to Much and said that he would wager everything he had that the monk was carrying money, and that Much and Scarlett should check their bows as they might have to fight. The three men nocked their arrows, and prepared to spring their ambush.

When the monk finally rode up alongside Little John's hiding place, the big man jumped out, with his bow at full draw, the arrow pointed at the monk's chest. He commanded the astonished monk to stop or die. Little John explained that his master was "annoyed at missing his meal because of people's tardiness." The monk asked who Little John's master was, and Little John told him proudly, "Robin Hood." The monk sneered in contempt at the name. Much did not think much of the monk's attitude and loosed a blunted arrow into the arrogant monk's chest, knocking him backwards off his horse. On seeing the monk's apparent demise, his retinue immediately scattered and fled, except for the two grooms who held the reins of the monk's packhorses.

Little John, Scarlett, and Much accompanied the dazed and unwilling monk to where Robin waited. As was customary in those times, Robin pulled back the hood of his cloak in a gesture of openness when they met, but the monk refused to do likewise. Little John, incensed at this disrespectful gesture, reached out to pull down the monk's hood. Robin stepped forward and waved Little John away. He asked how many men the monk had had in his retinue, and when Little John told him "fifty," Robin ordered him to blow his horn.

Errol Flynn as Robin Hood and Olivia de Havilland as Maid Marian from *The Adventures of Robin Hood* (1938), arguably the most popular and influential Robin Hood movie to date. (Mary Evans Picture Library)

Seventy of Robin's men came running at the summons, all of them dressed in scarlet striped tunics. Surrounded by so many heavily armed outlaws, a larger force than even his own retinue, the monk had no choice but to accept Robin Hood's invitation to dine with the Merry Men.

When they were all washed and seated to dinner, Robin opened the conversation by asking, "To which Abbey do you belong, and for whom do you work?"

The monk replied he was from St. Mary's and that the High Cellarer was his superior. That reminded Robin of the unpaid debt due him from the still-absent Sir Richard. He brought this to the attention of the monk and Little John added that the monk probably carried enough money to repay it. The monk insisted that he had never heard of Sir Richard of the Lea, or his debt, but Robin cut him off.

"You're a servant of the Church, and it is surely fate that you should show up at this fortuitous time." He then asked the monk how much money he carried. The monk replied that he only had 20 Marks on him. "If that's true," said Robin, "you may keep it and be on your way with my good wishes."He then ordered Little John to check the monk's baggage. Little John then spread the monk's cloak out on the ground. It was a matter of moments before the big man found a purse containing 800 pounds. Little John shouted out his discovery to Robin who was delighted with his windfall. Robin took the money, and, having no further use for the monk, sent him away with a note for the Abbot, asking him to send him a monk every day.

Sir Richard of the Lea finally rode into the Merry Men's territory shortly after the monk had departed. He greeted Robin warmly as he dismounted. Robin inquired of Sir Richard's land, and the knight replied that his land was safely back in his hands thanks to Robin. He added that he would have arrived sooner if he had not been held up by a wrestling match. Without further ado, the knight proffered the 400 pounds he owed Robin, plus 20 Marks as a courtesy payment. Robin was overjoyed, but declined the money, telling Sir Richard that the Church had already paid his debt, and he could not take it twice.

In addition, Robin gave Sir Richard the extra 400 pounds he had taken from the monk, and told him to use it wisely so that he would never be indebted again.

Little John and the Sheriff

It was on one of those perfect days when young men go out to shoot arrows for sport and wagers that Little John came to the attention of the Sheriff of Nottingham. At an impromptu tournament, Robin Hood's lieutenant had beaten the scores of a group of local Nottingham lads with three shots. The Sheriff, who had been watching nearby, was suitably impressed, and called him over. He asked John his name and where he was from.

Little John fighting the cook as depicted by Howard Pyle.

Little John warily gave a false name, "Reynold Greenleaf of Holderness," and the Sheriff seemed satisfied. He offered Little John a place in his retinue, for which "Reynold" would receive 20 Marks annually.

Little John was already in the service to the famous outlaw at the time but the Sheriff was able to persuade him to give his services for 12 months. Little John was happy to take the Sheriff's money, but he had no intention of becoming one of his faithful minions.

One Wednesday morning shortly thereafter, Little John lay in bed longer than he usually did. The Sheriff was away hunting and there was not much for Little John to do. It was after noon before hunger got the better of him, and he went down to the kitchens to ask for something to eat. The steward there refused to provide any food, however, unless his master was at home.

Little John threatened the steward, but the man ignored him and turned to leave. Angered by the steward's disrespect, Little John knocked him down, before helping himself to some food and drink. Several people in the kitchen witnessed this, and it so happened that one witness was a very large cook. He was affronted at Little John's behavior. The cook thought "Reynold's" act was very unjust, and that he was one of the Sheriff's worst bullies. The cook rushed over and punched him three times, prompting Little John to draw his sword. The cook reached for a nearby sword too, and the men squared up to fight.

Little John and the cook slashed and thrust at each other with their swords, the clanging of steel echoing in the kitchen. Little John was surprised at the cook's sword-fighting skills, and his sense of justice.

Pausing in the fight, John held up a hand, and told the cook, "If you can draw a bow as well as you wield a sword, I'll take you to join Robin Hood, and make you one of his Merry Men. Robin will give you 20 Marks annually and two changes of clothes."

The cook was tempted and said that if Little John sheathed his sword, the two would be friends. Little John complied, and, to confirm their new friendship, the cook prepared them both a meal of deer, bread, and wine. Over this repast, Little John and the cook made their plans to leave Nottingham that night. When darkness fell, the two new friends quietly made their way to the treasury and broke open the locks. Once inside, they took the Sheriff's silverware, including his silver chalice, and 300 pounds in cash, then fled into the woods.

By morning, when they reached the outlaw stronghold in the forest, Robin Hood was there to meet them. He was delighted to see Little John, his companion, and their acquisitions. He asked them for news of Nottingham, and Little John briefly recounted his adventure in the Sheriff's service. At this point, a plan came to Little John, which he told Robin would yield greater profit.

He abruptly turned and left, running as swiftly as he could through the forest, to a glade where the Sheriff of Nottingham was still out hunting. The Sheriff was also happy to see Little John, but asked why he had come so hastily. Little John replied, "I was walking in the forest when I saw a spectacular stag leading a herd of 70 deer through a clearing. The stag's antlers," he continued, "were so fearsome that I was afraid to attack it on my own."

The Sheriff grew excited at the prospect of such a prize and ordered Little John to lead the way. They ran back the way "Reynold" had come, the Sheriff's thoughts filled with the taste of venison and the image of a magnificent 12-pointer hanging on his wall.

"Just through here," John said, and the Sheriff ran faster, but instead of a stag standing in the clearing when they emerged from the trees, it was Robin Hood who waited, with his bow drawn and an arrow nocked. The Sheriff realized suddenly, and to his utter dismay, that he had been betrayed by "Reynold Greenfleaf," who Robin greeted warmly as Little John.

Little John fights the Sheriff's cook (opposite)

One famous tale has Little John infiltrate the Sheriff's household as a huntsman and archer. Howard Pyle correctly has the Sheriff living in a house in the town of Nottingham; he didn't live in the Castle. Hunting was available very close to hand, as a deer park, an enclosed area of land kept well stocked with animals to hunt, lay beneath the stone outcrop of the castle in an area still known today as "The Park."

One hunting morning, Little John wakes late and finds that the hunting party has left. He stumbles down to the kitchen and demands breakfast of the steward. The steward tells him that he's too late. John, true to character, creates a violent scene and grabs a chicken which he is about to eat when the cook, who is his equal in shortness of temper, enters the room, retrieves the chicken and draws his sword. Why a cook would wear a sword in his own kitchen is never explained, but there follows a mighty fight.

Neither can gain the upper hand and eventually they call it quits and become friends, quite a normal outcome of a fight in the tales. John declares himself to be Robin's man and invites the cook to join the famous outlaw band, which he accepts. They load up the Sheriff's silver plate onto their horses and set out into the forest.

- Peter Dennis

Robin invited the Sheriff to share their supper, and added insult to injury by promising to serve him on his own stolen silverware. He also told the Sheriff his life was safe but ordered Little John to strip him of his finery and give him a green cloak to wear.

Robin then called his Merry Men to him so that the Sheriff could see that they all slept in their cloaks, and that he was being treated no differently. The Sheriff therefore spent an uncomfortable night on the hard ground, trying to sleep among the band of outlaws. The next morning, Robin told the Sheriff that he was to live with them for 12 months in the forest, where they would teach him how to be a just man. The Sheriff replied that he would rather Robin cut off his head than spend another night in the woods, but that if Robin let him go, he would be the outlaw leader's friend.

Robin accepted the agreement, but made the Sheriff swear an oath to never harm Robin or his men, and to always provide aid when asked. The Sheriff gave his promise, and was soon on his way, but, of course, he had no intention of keeping his word.

Robin Hood and the Archery Contest

Soon after his overnight stay with the Merry Men, the Sheriff of Nottingham sent out a call for the best archers in the north of England to compete at the butts in Nottingham. This would be the grandest tournament for archers, and the winner would receive a silver arrow with golden feathers. Robin Hood soon heard of the Sheriff's archery contest, as word had spread so widely that the news even reached the meeting place in the depths of his forest.

Robin couldn't resist such a contest and was confident he would win, but he was also wary about a possible trap being set by the Sheriff. He gathered his Merry Men to accompany him to the competition, where they would also find out if the

Different sources often depict specific Merry Men in slightly different ways, but probably none varies quite as widely as Will Scarlett; even his name often changes. As Will Scatheloke, he is sometimes depicted as a violent and hot-headed man. As Will Scarlett, he can sometimes be foppish as depicted here by Howard Pyle.

Sheriff's word, given after his recent capture by Robin, was to be trusted.

When Robin arrived in Nottingham, therefore, he did so with 140 bowmen at his back.

Archers from far and wide had entered the competition. Robin chose five of his men to compete, in addition to himself, and instructed the rest to be ready just in case the Sheriff was up to his old tricks. All the competitors were to take three shots in rotation. Little John, Scarlett, Much, and two other Merry Men named Reynold and Gilbert all shot well, but they were no match for Robin, who beat them all and took the prize.

Just as Robin had suspected, however, the competition was a trap. As he began to leave, the Sheriff's horns blew to signal an ambush. Guards rushed in to surround Robin and his men, as a furious Robin accused the Sheriff of betrayal and shouted that his promise given in the forest had obviously meant nothing. Even as Robin protested, however, the arrows were already flying. As the Sheriff's men closed in for the kill, the rest of the Merry Men also attacked. Men fell dead and wounded on both sides, but the outlaws' archery gradually proved superior, and the Sheriff's men slowly fell back.

The surrounded Merry Men broke free of the cordon the guards had formed, and made for the forest. Robin thought that the crisis was over, but, just as he was about to make his run for the safety of the treeline, he saw Little John fall with an arrow in his knee. He immediately turned to help his friend.

In considerable pain, Little John demanded that Robin finish him off to prevent the Sheriff from taking him alive for torture. Robin refused, telling Little John he would never do such a thing, even if all the gold in England were laid in a row for him. Instead, he hoisted his trusty lieutenant over his back and carried him as they fled into the forest.

The fleeing outlaws ran for their lives through the trees until they came to a castle surrounded by a double-ditch. A familiar face stood at the gate, Sir Richard of the Lea, whom Robin had saved from debt. The knight welcomed Robin with open arms and an offer of his protection against the Sheriff. Sir Richard waved Robin and his men inside the castle, then ordered the gates shut and the drawbridge pulled up. He told his guests to arm themselves, man the walls, and prepare themselves for a siege.

The Rescue of Sir Richard of the Lea

It did not take long for the Sheriff of Nottingham to gather his forces at the gates of the castle. When his men were encamped outside, he shouted up to Sir Richard that the knight was a traitor for sheltering the King's enemies. The knight replied that these were his lands, and the Sheriff should leave until the King had been asked to make a judgment on the matter. The Sheriff could not act against a nobleman on his own authority and had no choice but to abandon the siege and travel to London to speak to the King.

In the meantime, Robin left the castle and returned to the forest, where he was joined by Little John, once the big man had healed.

When he reached the Royal court, the Sheriff told the King his story of how he tried to maintain the King's peace against the outlaw Robin Hood, but that a knight was preventing him from doing so. He then claimed that the knight threatened to usurp the King in the north. The alarmed King responded that he would travel to Nottingham within the fortnight and deal personally with both Robin and the knight. The Sheriff decided not to wait for the King, however, before taking action. He immediately rode back to Nottingham, intent on taking down the upstart knight.

Sir Richard expected the King or his representative to bring the decision concerning his recent conflict with the Sheriff, and while he was waiting he went about his normal business. The nobleman was completely unsuspecting, therefore, of the Sheriff's intentions to pre-empt the King. Sir Richard was out hawking by the river near his castle when, without warning, the Sheriff's henchmen grabbed him, bound him hand and foot, and rode off to Nottingham with him as their captive.

When Sir Richard's Lady heard what had happened from the falconer who looked after the birds for him, she rode directly to find Robin Hood, to beg him to save her husband. She warned Robin to act quickly, because the kidnapping party was less than three miles away. Robin was furious at the dishonorable act the Sheriff had committed, and immediately summoned his Merry Men to muster. Robin vowed that any of them who failed to help rescue the knight would be expelled from his band. With all of his 140 men firmly on his side, Robin left the forest, on the trail of the Sheriff of Nottingham.

The famous Shakespearian actor Frederick Warde played Robin Hood in the stage play, *Runneymede* by William Greer Harrison. The play opened in New York in 1895 and proved a dismal failure, shutting after only a few weeks. (Library of Congress)

One of Howard Pyle's clearest depictions of Robin Hood.

By marching quickly through the hidden forest paths only they knew, the Merry Men were able to outpace the Sheriff's men and reach Nottingham just in time to greet the Sheriff's party as they emerged from the trees with their prisoner. Robin stepped boldly in front of the Sheriff's horse and demanded to know what the King had said, but the Sheriff would not answer. Robin drew his bow and loosed an arrow into the Sheriff, knocking him from the saddle. He then drew his sword, and with a single, swift cut, severed the Sheriff's head, proclaiming that no man could trust him while he was still alive.

At that point, all the rest of the Merry Men drew their blades and attacked the Sheriff's retinue. Leaderless, the Sheriff's men were no match for the outlaw band and soon ran away from the fury of the Merry Men. When the last of them had fled, Robin walked over to Sir Richard and cut the rope that bound him.

He handed the knight a bow, telling him that, "For the moment, you must consider yourself an outlaw, and should return to the forest with the Merry Men. Hopefully," he added, "the King will soon show wisdom by pardoning you."

Robin Hood and the King

Two weeks later, the King arrived in Nottingham at the head of a procession of armed knights. When he learned of the death of the Sheriff, he immediately declared Sir Richard of the Lea an outlaw and stripped him of all his lands.

A Royal hunt was then organized, but deer were few and far between in the Royal forests, much to the annoyance of the King. He swore that he would find Robin Hood and that any man who brought him Sir Richard's head would receive the knight's forfeited lands as a reward.

At this, an old and more experienced knight stepped forward to gently remind the King that so long as Robin Hood carried a bow, no knight would be safe in Sir Richard's lands.

Over the next six months, the King's frustration grew. He stayed in Nottingham during that time, and every day brought new stories of Robin Hood stealing his deer with impunity. One day, a forester standing in the King's company suggested that, if he really wanted to face Robin Hood, he should dress five of his knights as monks, and then the forester would lead them to the outlaw. The King quickly agreed to the plan, and had five of his knights dressed in gray cowls. The King himself wore a broad-brimmed hat in the style of an Abbot. Thus suitably disguised, they made their way into the woods, led by the forester.

The Royal party had gone barely a mile into the trees when Robin Hood suddenly appeared in front of them. He grabbed the reins of the King's horse and politely introduced himself. Robin indicated his men, who now surrounded the travellers, and told the apparent Abbot that they were all yeomen down on their luck. Since the Church had so much, Robin pointed out, some charity was warranted. The disguised King replied that he only carried 40 pounds, but that Robin was welcome to it, as charity.

Robin gave half of this money to his men, and returned the other half to the Abbot for his expenses. The "Abbot" thanked Robin, then took out the King's Seal. He told Robin that he was a messenger from the King, ordered to find Robin and invite him to Nottingham. Robin dropped to his knees at the sight of the Seal and replied that he held no man in higher regard than the King. He thanked the Abbot for the invitation and, in return, requested him to have dinner in the forest.

Robin Hood and His Merry Men Entertaining Richard the Lionheart in Sherwood Forest by Daniel Maclise, painted in 1839. (Daniel Maclise/ Fine Art Photographic/Getty Images)

There is Pith in your arm said ROBIN HOOD

King Richard I visits Robin Hood in disguise in this drawing by the famed illustrator H. J. Ford.

Curious about the outlaw, the King accepted the invitation.

Robin led the disguised King's party into his forest camp, where venison was prepared for a feast. Then Robin blew his horn, beckoning his Merry Men. One hundred and forty of them – Sir Richard included – quickly gathered round the campfire. The King was surprised and impressed by the command that Robin had over his men. Without further ado, they all settled down to the feast of venison, bread, ale, and wine. This was as fine as anything the King was used to, and he felt quite at home with such a dinner. Afterwards, Robin wanted to show the "Abbot" how they lived in the forest. Robin's men immediately began to string their bows, making ready for an archery contest.

Robin explained that if his men missed their shots – at what the King thought was an extraordinary distance – they would forfeit their equipment for the day, and receive a knock on the head. When the contest started, Robin quickly proved the best shot, defeating everyone, including Will Scarlett and Little John. Then even Robin missed.

One of the Merry Men, Gilbert, turned to Robin and reminded him that he too was subject to the rules of the contest. Robin agreed that he was not above the rules and handed his arrows to the Abbot as a permission to deliver the blow. The King demurred at first, but Robin insisted. So the King rolled up his sleeve and punched Robin so hard that he nearly knocked the outlaw to the ground. The blow stunned Robin, and he became suspicious, believing it was the strike of a trained warrior. Robin and Sir Richard of the Lea examined their guest more closely, then fell to their knees in belated recognition, and the Merry Men followed suit.

The King, realizing the potential danger he was in from an outlaw band that outnumbered his party by more than 20 to one, asked for mercy. Robin immediately countered that it was he who begged for mercy from the King. The King, impressed by Robin's fairness as a leader, agreed – but only on the condition that Robin and his men left the forest and took service at the King's court. Robin said that he would serve the King, but even as he spoke, he suspected he would soon be back to hunting the Royal deer through the woods.

Robin Hood at the King's Court

Immediately following Robin Hood's acceptance of the King's offer to enter Royal service, the King asked him if he had any green cloth to sell, since he had had enough of the clerical robes of his disguise. Robin, of course, had 33 yards of Lincoln green that he was happy to part with, and the King and his men were soon dressed in it and ready to go back to Nottingham. Robin and the King also competed in archery contests, with Robin again impressing the King with his accuracy.

As they approached Nottingham, all in Lincoln green, however, people there began to panic, fearing that Robin had killed the King and had come to wreak his revenge. Hastily, the King and his knights stepped forward to quell the citizens' fears. That night, once they were all settled in at the castle there, the King pardoned Sir Richard of the Lea, and gave him back his lands. All appeared well at the King's court.

Robin stayed 15 months in the King's service and gained great renown for his upstanding conduct. His men began to drift off and return to their own lives, however, until only Little John and Will Scarlett remained. Robin grew sorrowful, lamenting the loss of his reputation as the best archer in England. He knew that he could no longer stay in the King's service, and that he must return to Barnesdale.

A mid-19th century depiction of Robin Hood, showing him in dress more appropriate to various continental European settings. (Richard Dadd/Getty Images)

Robin asked the King for permission to take seven days' leave in order to visit the chapel of Mary Magdalene on a pilgrimage. The King granted Robin his wish, and the grateful ex-outlaw left to travel north back to his forest. He arrived to the sound of birdsong, and Robin realized he had been gone too long. He also harbored a desire to shoot a deer, which he did before blowing his horn to let the outlaws of the forest know that their leader was back.

As the Merry Men celebrated Robin's visit, and Robin enjoyed the sounds and scents of the forest, he realized that he could not leave again, even to return to the service of the King. For the next 22 years, Robin would live in his forest, rarely leaving for fear of the King's revenge.

Robin Hood and Guy of Gisborne

Robin Hood was troubled by nightmares. He had awoken in the middle of the night from a dream in which two strong men had first bested him in a fight, then bound him and stolen his bow. He described this dream to Little John, saying that he felt he must seek out the two men. Little John dismissed the dreams as being flighty and meaningless and not messages or portents,

THE SHERIFF IS CAPTURED (OPPOSITE)

Later in the tale where Little John fights the cook, he catches up with the Sheriff hunting in the greenwood. Since the Sheriff has no knowledge of John's theft of his plate and still has confidence in him, it is a simple matter for John to lure him into a trap where he encounters Robin Hood and his band. He is treated to a feast in the camp off his own silverware, cooked by his own ex-cook.

Big old oaks in Sherwood grow huge horizontal branches, and I've always liked the idea of a treeful of outlaws. In the illustration, Little John takes a firm grip of the Sheriff's boar spear, and the Sheriff realizes that he's been tricked.

The Sheriff is captured many times in the tales and killed more than once, too. He's never named though, so he may be more than one corrupt and wicked man.

- Peter Dennis

but Robin would not be dissuaded. He mustered his men and told them that he and Little John were going off into the forest. Then the pair donned their green cloaks, picked up their bows, and walked off in search of the men from Robin's dream.

After a few hours, Robin and Little John spied an oddly dressed man leaning against a tree. The stranger wore a sword and dagger on his belt and had a bow in his hand, but what made him so unusual was his horsehide cloak, complete with head, tail, and mane. Little John suggested that Robin should hide while he investigated, but Robin was insulted by the suggestion.

"Do you think I'm afraid?" he demanded, "or that I can't take care of myself, that you would belittle me so? All I'm afraid of," he added, "is that I'd break my bow if I hit you with it – and that's the only reason I won't."

Astonished at this rebuke, Little John turned his back on Robin and stormed off towards Barnesdale.

Now alone, Robin approached the man leaning against the tree. By the look of the bow in his hand, Robin judged him to be an accomplished archer. The two exchanged greetings, and then Robin asked what brought the man to the forest. The stranger replied that he had come in search of Robin Hood. With a knowing grin, Robin suggested that the two have an archery contest, because, as everyone knew, such contests were sure to attract the famous outlaw. The stranger agreed and the targets were soon set.

Robin offered his opponent the first shot, but the stranger demurred, so Robin nocked his arrow and let fly. It was a bullseye, but then the stranger shot his arrow into the bullseye too. Robin loosed again, for another bullseye, but the stranger also did likewise again. Worse, this time the stranger's arrow was in the exact center of the bullseye, to the exact hairsbreadth. There seemed to be no way in which Robin could beat such a shot, but the outlaw, undeterred, shot again.

This time, Robin's third arrow split the stranger's arrow right down the center. The stranger had proved no match for Robin and gave up in disgust.

The stranger turned to this great archer who had beaten him, and asked his name, but Robin refused to give it until the stranger revealed his.

Robin Hood battles Guy of Gisborne. Artwork by Peter Dennis.

"Guy of Gisborne," the man replied, and he went on to say that, "I have come into the forest to capture the outlaw, Robin Hood."

Robin then introduced himself and drew his sword. Guy of Gisborne did likewise, and, sweating in the summer heat, the two men stood toe to toe, slashing and thrusting at each other, with neither man giving any ground as they circled each other, looking for an advantage. Suddenly, Robin tripped over a tree root and tumbled to the ground. In a flash, Guy of Gisborne lunged forward and pierced Robin on his left side as he desperately tried to roll away. Bleeding heavily from the wound, Robin leapt to his feet and delivered a backhanded slash that bit deep into Guy of Gisborne, who fell, dead before his body hit the ground.

Robin grabbed Gisborne by the hair and cut off his head, which he then stuck on the end of his bow. He also slashed the dead man's face to make him unrecognizable. Finally, Robin exchanged his clothes, put on the horseshide cloak, and picked up Guy's bow and hunting horn.

While Robin and Guy were fighting it out, Little John made his way back to Barnesdale. When he arrived, however, he found two of the Merry Men lying dead. Little John stopped to examine the bodies, but as he did so a group of the Sheriff's men attacked. A new Sheriff had been appointed, and Nottingham's guards had not forgotten the crime committed by his predecessor. Little John jumped up and began to run, pausing only to shoot down one of his pursuers. There were too many of them, however, and their horses were faster than a man on foot. Little John was quickly run down and captured. The Sheriff's men tied Little John to a tree, just as the new Sheriff himself rode up. The Sheriff, delighted at the capture of Robin Hood's right-hand man, commanded that Little John be immediately taken away and executed on a nearby high hill.

Before the guards could move to drag Little John off to the gallows hill, a horn sounded in the forest. The Sheriff smiled, recognizing the signal of Guy of Gisborne, the man he had hired to hunt down his predecessor's killer. A few moments later, he saw the bounty hunter approaching, clad in his distinctive horsehide cloak, and carrying a gruesomely-mutilated severed head on the end of his bow. The Sheriff shouted out a greeting, and proclaimed that Guy could have any reward he named. The man in the horsehide cloak laughed, and asked only that now that he had taken the head of Robin Hood, that he should be allowed to kill his lieutenant, Little John, as well.

The Sheriff agreed, and waved his men to force Little John to his knees before the bounty hunter. The Sheriff hurried towards the two men, keen to see the outlaw die at the hand of his hired man, but instead of killing Little John, the man in horsehide cut the big man's ropes and handed him a bow. On seeing this, the astonished Sheriff realized he'd been deceived. He was now close enough to more clearly see the bounty hunter's features and immediately saw through Robin Hood's disguise.

As the outlaws loosed shafts into his guards, the Sheriff wheeled his horse around, and started off into a gallop, but his bid to escape was in vain. Little John drew a bead on the Sheriff and sent an arrow straight into his heart through his back.

The post of Sheriff of Nottingham was vacant once more.

Robin Hood and the Monk

It was a glorious Sunday morning and Little John was full of the joys of Spring. Robin Hood, on the other hand, was feeling more troubled because he had not been to Mass for over two weeks. Perhaps because he had certain sins to confess, Robin decided that he must go into Nottingham to attend services. Much the Miller's Son suggested to Robin that he take a dozen well-armed bodyguards along, but Robin would only allow Little John to accompany him.

As they walked through the woods on their way to Nottingham, Robin and Little John got into a heated argument over an old gambling debt. Little John claimed to have won five shillings from Robin, which was still owed from months earlier, but Robin said this had never happened. Unable to control himself as Little John persisted in his claim, Robin struck Little John on the head. John drew his sword and declared that if Robin were not his master and

This woodcut of Robin Hood presents him in 16th century dress. For reasons unknown, he is wearing spurs. He is firing an arrow at a strangely shaped tower, which is possibly meant to represent a tower of Nottingham Castle. (Mary Evans Picture Library / Alamy)

his friend, he would have run him through for that. Robin refused to apologize, let alone pay the gambling debt, and so the two men parted company. Little John stormed off into the trees and Robin continued alone to Nottingham.

When he reached Nottingham, Robin quickly made his way to St. Mary's Church. As he knelt to pray, however, a nearby monk recognized the outlaw as the man who had previously robbed him of 100 pounds of Church funds. Sure that Robin hadn't noticed him, the monk sprinted out of the church and ran to find the Sheriff. When the Sheriff heard what the monk had to say, he immediately mustered his men to arms and hurried to the church.

The Sheriff's men crashed through the doors of the church with drawn swords. The commotion at the doors drew Robin from his prayers and turned his brain and instincts to the imminent danger. Despite being massively outnumbered, and since there were no other exits, Robin charged desperately into the soldiers, cutting his way directly for the Sheriff. Twelve men fell to Robin's sword and many others were wounded, but the outlaw's luck ran out when his sword broke over the Sheriff's helmet. Suddenly disarmed, Robin was overwhelmed and taken prisoner.

Word of the fight, and of Robin's capture, spread like wildfire, and the news soon reached the Merry Men. They quickly held a council of war, and Little John, who had returned just before the shocking news, immediately exclaimed that he would go into Nottingham and rescue Robin. The rest of the

Merry Men, however, backed away from him, suspicious and angry that he had abandoned Robin and left him to the Sheriff's mercies. In the end, only Much the Miller's Son stood forward and said he would go with Little John.

The two outlaws first made their way to Much's uncle's house, which stood alongside the highway to Nottingham, with a view to ambushing travellers in order to secure their clothes as a disguise. No one suitable passed that day or night, but, the following morning, Little John spied a familiar monk riding along the road with his young page. He alerted Much and the two men stayed hidden and silent until the monk came close enough to intercept. When he did, the pair leapt out into the road to greet the startled monk.

"Is it true that the outlaw Robin Hood has been captured?" Little John asked. "If so, it's about time, as he robbed me of 20 Marks, and I should be glad of that news."

"Yes," the monk replied. "I too had been robbed by him, and so recognized him at once. If you were also his victims, you should thank me for being the first to lay hands on the outlaw. Indeed, my page and I are just now riding to tell the King of the news."

Little John thanked the monk, and then said, "Robin may be captured, but the woods are still filled with his Merry Men. Why don't my friend and I accompany you on your journey, to deter any of those robbers that might be lying in wait?" The monk accepted gladly, seeing the sense in having two tough-looking warriors with him.

Little John strode off down the road, leading the monk's horse by its bridle, so that the monk couldn't ride it away. Much, meanwhile, walked with the monk's page, to prevent any possible escape by the boy. They travelled just far enough to be out of sight and sound of any possible travellers, and to lull the monk into a false sense of security, when Little John suddenly grabbed the monk by his hood, and threw him roughly to the ground. He shouted down at the monk that Robin Hood was his master and his friend and that the monk would not be delivering more messages to the King.

Then Little John swiftly drew his sword and sliced off the monk's head. Before the page could so much as scream, Much cut off his head too. The outlaws quickly stripped their victims, donned their cowls, and buried the bodies in shallow graves. They then hurried off to deliver the news to the King themselves.

Little John was taken to the King the moment he appeared at the Royal court. He knelt and handed over the letters that he had taken from the dead monk. The King was delighted with the news of Robin Hood's capture, but asked Little John about the whereabouts of the monk who was supposed to deliver the letter. "He died on the road," Little John replied simply. Satisfied with that answer, the King gave Little John and Much 20 pounds for their trouble and made them yeomen of the Crown.

More importantly, he also gave Little John his Royal Seal to take to the Sheriff of Nottingham, along with an order to return to the court with Robin Hood.

The first actor to portray Robin Hood on television was Patrick Troughton, in a 1953 BBC miniseries entitled *Robin Hood*. Troughton is now better remembered for being the second actor to portray Doctor Who. (© BBC/Corbis)

Much and Little John made their way quickly back to Nottingham, but found the gates closed and barred. They asked the porter at the gatehouse why this was and received the answer that, because Robin Hood was in prison, revenge attacks by Little John, Much, and Scarlett were killing men along the walls every day.

Little John didn't betray any surprise that he and Much were supposedly attacking Nottingham when they were travelling with the Royal Seal, but instead demanded to see the Sheriff, explaining that he was on an errand from the King. When he saw the Royal Seal, the porter let John and Much in through the gatehouse and led them to the Sheriff. When the Sheriff saw the King's seal, he asked what had happened to the monk who had taken the original message.

"The King was so grateful for the news," Little John told him with a straight face, "that he made the monk Abbot of Westminster."

The delighted Sheriff threw a party with wine and ale for all, and it was well into the small hours of the morning when they all retired for the night. But Little John and Much only pretended to sleep drunkenly. When they were certain everyone else was dead to the world, they stole down to the prison and called for the jailer, shouting, "Robin Hood is gone! The outlaw has escaped!"

When the alarmed jailer came running to check on Robin and query his visitors, Little John pinned him to the wall with his sword. The big man took the keys from the body of the jailer and freed Robin without further incident.

Hurrying quietly past the ale-befuddled guards, the three outlaws escaped over the walls and fled into the night.

Once they were safely away, Little John turned to Robin Hood and said he was leaving the Merry Men. He had repaid any debt he might owe, he added. Robin refused to hear this, though, and even offered Little John the leadership of the Merry Men, if only he would stay. Little John had no desire to be a leader, but Robin's generous offer touched him, and he decided that he would after all remain in Robin's service.

Friends once more, the two outlaws and Much continued through the woods until they reached their stronghold. With the Merry Men once more gathered all together as a united band of comrades, they celebrated the return of their leader and his lieutenant long into the night with a huge feast.

The Myth of Robin Hood

In May 1515, King Henry VIII, his Queen, Catherine of Aragon, and their court retinue of lords and ladies rode out to Shooter's Hill in London. As they approached their destination, a company of hooded yeomen dressed in green and armed with bows and arrows intercepted the Royal entourage. Their commander stepped forward and proclaimed that he was Robin Hood and asked permission to demonstrate his men's archery skills to the King. Henry granted the request, as planned, and an entertaining afternoon was had by all, followed by a sumptuous feast of deer and wine at Robin's table in a nearby green wood.

The archers, of course, were men of the King's bodyguard, but the importance of the event was that the Robin Hood legend, far from its humble beginnings, had met with Royal approval. Not coincidentally, it was around this time that Robin Hood began to make his way into print and became a character in the popular May Games.

May Games festivals were part of the agricultural social calendar throughout the Medieval period. They involved feasting and entertainments, dancing and drinking and could easily descend into chaos. The spirit of the games seems to have been driven by a desire to break out from the strict rhythms of medieval life, if only for one day. It is hardly surprising, therefore, that as his legend spread, Robin Hood would make an appearance at the May Games.

By the end of the 15th century he was a common sight, and thus Robin became more widely known. The May Games may also be the source of Maid Marian. Although Marian doesn't appear in the original legends or even most of the later Myths, she may have derived from the position of May Queen, who was a standard character in the celebrations.

A woodcut illustration depicting Robin, Maid Marian, Friar Tuck and other members of the Merry Men. (Mary Evans Picture Library)

The May Games also generated the first plays based on the Robin Hood character. However, the reworking of the Robin Hood legend through plays also led to a change in his public persona, and to the creation of the myth. In the 16th and 17th centuries, Robin's story was spread through single-sheet "broadsides," or small, cheap booklets. Their sales were helped by increased literacy, which meant a widening audience. However, with so few original stories to draw from, these latter day balladeers embellished them with new characters and events.

Moreover, with the changes in readership wrought by cultural developments, Robin's character had to literally change with the times. Thus, by 1820, Walter Scott, in his novel *Ivanhoe*, had completely transformed Robin into a noble exile pining for the return of Richard the Lionheart from the Crusades to replace the evil usurper, King John. Scott drew from threads already forming in the Robin Hood story, as seen in the collected works known as the Percy Folio, but his immense popularity helped sew the tradition into a new fabric that, with few changes, remains to this day.

Robin Hood and Little John meet for the first time by Howard Pyle.

Robin Hood and Little John

The days before Robin had first met Little John had been a lean time for Robin Hood and his band of Merry Men. They had gone weeks without intercepting a suitable target for robbery, and so it was up to their leader to drum up some business. Robin gathered his men in a grove to tell them his plans and promised that if he got into too much difficulty he would blow on his horn for help.

With much shaking of hands and goodbyes, Robin picked up his bow and walked away into the forest, to find out why no suitable victims had come this way in such a long time.

Robin had not gone far into the woods when he spotted a very large man, standing in his path. The man stood on a narrow bridge across a wide and deep stream, and he held a quarterstaff in his hands. Robin politely asked the man to stand aside and let him pass, but the giant did not move. Robin stepped back to draw an arrow from his quiver. Before the arrow was even in Robin's hand, however, the large man growled a warning at him.

"If that arrow so much as touches string, I'll give you a ducking."

Robin laughed at such effrontery. "Do you think you can outpace an arrow? I could shoot you down before you ever got close enough to use that staff."

The man gripped his staff tighter, and retorted, "Only a coward threatens a man at the point of bow and arrow."

Robin flushed with anger, and declared, "No man calls me a coward and lives."

With that, he put down his bow and walked over to a nearby thicket of young oak trees to select a suitable branch to be his staff.

The outlaw leader was soon ready to fight the big man. The two closed and darted out quick blows at each other, which were easily parried, before Robin dealt the first jarring blow to the other man's ribs. The shock of Robin's successful attack spurred the giant on to greater efforts, and he advanced anew. The two combatants lashed out against each other with their staves, both seeking the opening for the decisive hit.

The big stranger struck home next, catching Robin across the head and drawing blood. The dazed Robin, now thoroughly enraged, flew into a blind frenzy of swings and lunges with his staff, and the sparring grew ever more intense, until, finally, Robin's anger led him to err, and the furious stranger hit Robin across the back, knocking him clear off the bridge.

Robin Hood statue outside of Nottingham Castle. Photographed by Mike Peel. (www.mikepeel.net)

The stranger drew back his staff and looked over the side of the bridge. He broke into laughter.

"Where have you gone?" he called out. "Are you tired out already?"

"Down here," Robin replied, "cooling my head in the water. I fear I have to concede defeat."

He pulled himself out of the brook by grabbing hold of an overhanging thorn bush, then blew a loud blast on his horn. The horn's call brought the Merry Men running through the woods to their leader.

"Why are you soaked?" one of them asked Robin.

Robin replied that, "This fellow knocked me into the brook."

The Merry Men swarmed on to the bridge and grabbed the giant before he could react.

"He could use a wash himself," they cried, dragging the big man to the edge.

Just as the outlaws were about to dunk the stranger into the brook, Robin had a change of heart, and called out, "Stop!" He told the stranger that, "No one will hurt a man who won a bout fair and square."

Then, reminding his men that they could always use someone who was so handy in a fight, Robin offered the man a place in his band, along with everything he might need to live in the forest with the outlaws. The offer included a bow and lessons on how to use it. The stranger immediately accepted the olive branch and promised to obey Robin's command. He then introduced himself as John Little.

Robin and Little John on the Bridge (opposite)

In this painting, the young Robin Hood set out from the outlaw camp for a lone ramble through the forest and encountered the hulking and combative John Little on a log bridge. His first instinct was to draw his bow, but John persuaded him to lay it aside and cut himself a quarterstaff to make the contest equal. Robin, as usual, is bested and gets a ducking, but this was just the beginning of his stormy relationship with his most trusted and most quarrelsome henchman.

No set of Robin Hood illustrations could be complete without a treatment of this famous encounter. The simple bridge may have spanned the stream for fifty years and become overgrown. Robin, always over-confident in sporting combats with the local hard-men, quickly realizes that he's in hot water and will soon be in the cold stuff.

- Peter Dennis

Later, as the Merry Men were feasting in the forest with their new recruit, Will Scarlett offered to act as John Little's archery teacher. He added with a touch of irony, that in respect of his size, they should call the new outlaw "Little John." Robin gave the newly christened Merry Man some new green clothes and a huge bow. He then told Little John of the history of the Merry Men and of their free-living lifestyle. The presentation concluded, the men returned to their feast and celebrated well into the night.

The Jolly Pinder of Wakefield

Robin Hood, Will Scarlett, and Little John went on a visit to Wakefield. As they approached the town gates, they heard the town pinder claim that not even a knight or squire could enter the town without his permission. This was a bold claim for a pinder, whose actual job was to round up stray animals, though they sometimes took on the mantle of a local keeper of law and order.

The pinder was sitting under a thorn-bush, and so was unaware of the approach of three outlaws from the forest until Robin cleared his throat. The pinder looked up in surprise at his visitors, but quickly composed himself and told them to turn around, because they had come over the cornfields and thus avoided the King's highway and his toll. Robin Hood laughed, pointing out that the pinder was outnumbered three to one, but the pinder was made of sterner stuff than his oafish bragging might otherwise have suggested.

Drawing his sword, the pinder stood with his back to the thorn-bush, and set his foot on a large stone. The three outlaws needed no further invite; they held tight their bucklers and drew their swords. They launched themselves at the pinder, but the fight did not go according to Robin's plan. The pinder fought hard, parrying the outlaws' attacks and giving as good as he got in return. Because he had the thorn-bush at his back, they could not surround or outflank him, and so their numerical advantage was somewhat neutralized.

On and on the fight went, into the heat of the summer's day, until Robin finally called a halt.

Robin Hood and the Beggar. Beggars frequently appear in the stories of Robin Hood and very often turn out to be tougher than they look. In the most famous tale, Robin Hood beats a beggar in a fight, then borrows his clothes so he can try out the lifestyle. Artwork by Peter Dennis.

"This must be the toughest pinder in England," he exclaimed. He then offered the official a place among the Merry Men.

The pinder readily accepted the offer. "I have no love nor loyalty for my current master," he told Robin, "but I must stay until after Michaelmas, when I will receive my pay." Robin was agreeable to the pinder's compromise. The men shared some bread and ale at the gatehouse, and then Robin and his companions said their goodbyes to the pinder, until they would meet again in the forest.

Robin Hood and the Curtal Friar

On a perfect day in the forest, Robin Hood's Merry Men were in high spirits, taking the time for sport as well as to practice their archery skills. Robin, Much the Miller's Son, Little John, and Will Scarlett decided to hunt deer, but at the same time to show off their bowmanship to each other. They soon began to stalk a likely herd of deer, and Will Scarlett lined up the first shot.

Scarlett brought down a buck with his first arrow, then Much killed a doe with another. Little John topped both of them, however, by piercing the heart of a deer at a range of 500 feet. Robin was so impressed by Little John's shooting that he said he would ride 100 miles to see a shot as good as that one.

Will Scarlett laughed. "No need to ride quite so far," he said. "I know of a friar at Fountains Abbey who could beat both of you and all the Merry Men."

"Prove it," Robin replied, and he swore that he would neither eat nor drink until he had seen for himself what the friar could do. Gathering 50 men from their camp, Robin and the others set off for Fountains Abbey.

As they approached the Abbey grounds, Robin stationed his men in a stand of ferns, commanding them to listen for the sound of his horn. He then carried on alone, until he came to a fast flowing river near the Abbey. Robin moved along the riverbank until he found a convenient ford, and there he spotted a friar. Robin asked for the friar's help in crossing the river, because he was a weary traveller.

The first meeting between Robin Hood and Friar Tuck is reputed to have taken place near Fountains Abbey in North Yorkshire. (PD)

The charitable friar happily took Robin Hood onto his back and carried him across. Once they reached the other side, however, the friar recognized the outlaw. Drawing his sword, the friar ordered Robin to carry him back. Robin had no choice but to obey and waded back through the water with the friar on his back. When he put the friar down, Robin quickly drew his own sword and demanded to be carried back across the river a second time.

The friar pretended to fear the outlaw's sword, and, with a mischievous gleam in his eye, presented his back for Robin to climb on. This time, though, when the friar reached the middle of the ford, he suddenly dumped Robin off his back and into the deeper part of the river.

"Now you have a choice of crossings: sink or swim."

Robin swam to the bank where he'd left his bow, while the friar walked back to the same bank and grabbed his buckler. Robin loosed an arrow, which stuck in the friar's shield. The friar laughed and told Robin, "You can shoot all day if you want, I can collect all your arrows." Robin drew another arrow and loosed, then another, and another. The friar's shield caught or deflected them all.

Out of ammunition, Robin drew his sword and advanced upon the friar. For six hours, the two men exchanged blows, splashing back and forth across the riverbank until the exhausted Robin could take no more and fell to his knees. Gasping for air, he begged a moment's truce. The friar granted his request, drawing back warily from his assailant. Robin quickly grabbed his horn and blew three blasts on it.

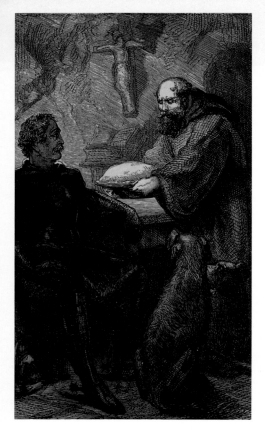

Friar Tuck and Richard the Lionheart from a 19th century edition of Walter Scott's *Ivanhoe*. (PD_US)

Almost immediately, the Merry Men appeared, drawn by their leader's signal, with their weapons drawn and ready for action. The friar, who had expected the outlaw to have no more than a couple of men with him, realized that he had made a grave tactical error. He asked Robin for permission to whistle for help of his own. With so many of his men behind him, Robin was not worried by any threats coming from the friar, so he granted the request.

The friar put his fingers to his mouth and whistled. Soon, 50 fierce hunting-dogs bounded up to the combatants, circling around the Merry Men.

The friar turned to Robin, and said, "I have a dog for each of your forest wolves."

"I'd rather face three dogs or three wolves than spend more hours fighting you," Robin replied, "but if you hold your dogs at bay, I'd rather count you a friend than shed either of our blood."

The friar whistled again and the dogs lay down. Robin offered the friar a place among his Merry Men for which he would pay a Noble and guarantee a change of clothes on every holy day thereafter. The friar, whose name was Tuck, accepted Robin's generous offer and left Fountains Abbey with him to join the outlaw band.

Robin Hood and the Bishop

The sun was shining bright in the forest on the day that Robin Hood completely fooled a bishop and took the man for every penny he had. Robin had begun the day with a walk through the woods, looking for a way to pass the time. Through the trees, he saw a flash of metal and went to investigate. Spying from the undergrowth near a road through the forest, he saw a bishop in all his finery, accompanied by a large retinue of monks, grooms, pages, and guards. Alone, and on the wrong side of this armed force from his Merry Men, Robin decided that discretion was the better part of valor.

Nearby was a small cottage where an old woman lived. Robin had once given her shoes and warm clothes when the winter was cold. Robin ran to the cottage to ask the woman for help. The old woman was naturally suspicious of this stranger and asked who he was.

"It's Robin Hood," he said, and she recognized her benefactor's voice at once. With no time to lose, Robin told her that he needed her assistance to get around the Bishop and his entourage. Robin and the woman quickly changed clothes, so that Robin wore the woman's gray cloak, and she wore his customary Lincoln green.

Disguised as the old woman, Robin was able to slip past the Bishop's men without arousing their suspicion. Once past them, he ran back to where his Merry Men were camped.

The Bishop's men, meanwhile, had arrived at the old woman's house, where the Bishop caught sight of a figure in Lincoln green skulking around. Thinking that he had spotted Robin Hood, he sent his men into the cabin to seize the notorious outlaw. The guards rushed forward and burst into the cabin, where they found a figure with a green hood drawn down over its face. Thinking it was Robin, the Bishop's men bound the old woman's hands behind her and bustled her out of the cabin.

When they emerged from the cabin, dragging their still hooded captive behind them, the Bishop was so delighted that he ordered his prisoner thrown onto a white horse without checking to make sure it actually was who he thought it was. Delighted at the reward they would be able to claim, the Bishop's men turned for home.

As the Bishop and his retinue rode, they noticed an increasing rustling in the woods all around, which made them nervous. Suddenly, 100 bowmen appeared all around, some standing on the ground, others balancing in the branches of the trees. The startled Bishop demanded to know the identity of these newcomers. To his considerable surprise, the answer came from his captive.

"I think you'll find it might be Robin Hood and his Merry Men."

"But you're Robin Hood," the Bishop exclaimed, pulling the hood from his prisoner's head. When he saw that the face under the hood was that of an old woman, the Bishop, now thoroughly confused, asked his captive who she was.

Robin Hood himself then stepped out in front of his men, saying, "Why, it's the old woman who lives in the cabin near the road, of course."

While the Merry Men helped the old woman down, Robin took control of the Bishop's horse and tied it to a tree. He then took the Bishop's mantle and laid it on the ground, before emptying the Bishop's purses and saddlebags on top of it. The total haul came to 500 pounds, which his men swiftly bore away.

A woodcut of Robin and his men robbing the Bishop. (Mary Evans Picture Library / Alamy)

His business done, Robin ordered the Bishop released. Little John had a more amusing idea, however, and suggested that the Bishop be tied to the tree as well, so that he could sing the Merry Men a Mass. The bishop had no choice and said Mass for the outlaws, but one last indignity remained. When the Mass was over, Robin sat the bound Bishop backwards on his horse and handed him the horse's tail.

Thus humiliated, the Bishop was free to go.

THE OUTLAW LIFE

A 1920 illustration of Robin Hood and his men poaching a dear from the King's Forest. (Ivy Close Images / Alamy)

Even though we do not know precisely when Robin Hood lived, he certainly did so during violent times. Indeed, outlaws like Robin and his Merry Men helped generate a hostile environment that ebbed and flowed throughout the Middle Ages. Moreover, people then, as now, worried about rising crime rates, and differing methods and processes were deployed to tighten up on law and order. That was often easier said than done, however, because of the periodic political disruptions that led to civil unrest and sometimes open warfare. It is instructive that two periods often associated with Robin Hood, the 1260s and 1320s, witnessed open rebellions against the Crown followed by a turbulent aftermath.

A second factor in driving men to crime was the state of the economy, and, in particular, the quality of the harvest. Adding to the problem was the fact that corruption among local officials could produce more problems than those outside the law. In such circumstances, outlaws became instruments of unofficial justice and were lauded as heroes by the powerless and downtrodden, of which there were many.

Although ballads like those celebrating Robin Hood often make the outlaw life seem glamorous, the truth was that being an outlaw was an extremely precarious existence. Only men could be declared outlaw, presumably because only men had enough legal rights to be deprived of them.

The punishment was also much worse than it sounds because outlaws had no rights at all. The word "outlaw" itself meant that a man had been placed outside of the protection of the law, meaning he could receive no help from anyone, as helping an outlaw was illegal, and that anyone could kill him with impunity. There was no punishment for killing an outlaw. There were, moreover, bounties for capturing outlaws, who would then more often than not face the hangman's noose. However, local officials could not be too free with the rope for fear of stirring civil unrest; thus, it was often in their best interests to pardon an outlaw or accept payment of a fine. Also, of course, men hanging at the end of ropes could not line the pockets of corrupt officials out to enrich themselves.

Outlaws banded together for protection as well as to carry out more crimes, and they did so as far away as possible from the civil society that had rejected them. A forest as large and wild as Sherwood was an ideal defensible refuge for an outlaw gang such as the Merry Men. This was particularly true for outlaws who had been refused a pardon or who could not afford to pay a fine or a bribe.

Organized gangs could create serious headaches for local authorities. In the 1320s, the Folville and Coterel gangs terrorized the North Midlands during the chaotic collapse of Edward II's reign and in the wake of the failed rebellion of Thomas of Lancaster. Both gangs caused mayhem for the usual reasons of greed and local power, but, on at least one occasion, the Coterels acted on behalf of their local cathedral chapter at Lichfield.

Clerical involvement in crime was relatively common in the Medieval period. Robin Hood's confrontations with clerics and bishops would have been welcomed by many in a time when the Church was given so many privileges, and its officials could sidestep the law so easily. Abuse of power and patronage was rife among senior clergy, and many employed violent methods to further their temporal ambitions.

Ultimately, there were many men in the 13th and 14th centuries like Robin Hood, and perhaps one who originally operated under that name managed to spark a legend. It was an era when it was relatively easy to fall foul of the law and therefore be outlawed, especially when many local law enforcement officials were as corrupt as the sheriffs of Nottingham in the legend and myth. Once outlawed, Robin's life was all but forfeit, and he took to the forest where he met men in similar desperate situations. He became their leader, and his gang, the Merry Men, lived off the land through poaching and acquired wealth by deploying violence and robbery against the Sheriff and corrupt Church officials.

However, as the legend tells us, Robin Hood enforced stringent rules about who was a legitimate target and who should be left unmolested. That he did not take from the rich to give to the poor, as is claimed in the myth, misses the point that Robin had standards and scruples; that he did not exploit the already overburdened lower classes. Honest men and women, first in England and now around the world, have understood, respected, and, in the end, venerated the great outlaw's struggle ever since in their ballads, stories, plays, and most recently in movies and television series.

Robin Hood and Allan-a-Dale

One day, on his way to the meeting tree in the forest, Robin Hood noticed an excited young man in the distance, approaching through some fields. The stranger was dressed entirely in red, and was singing to himself as he skipped and danced his way across the fields and, eventually, out of sight.

Robin saw the stranger again the next morning, but this time the bright scarlet clothes, and the dancing, were gone, and the man trudged along, sighing and complaining to himself about some misfortune. Overcome by curiosity, Robin sent Little John and Much the Miller's Son after the man to investigate.

The stranger was wary at the approach of these two outlaws. He carried a bow, so he nocked an arrow in readiness, and asked the two newcomers to identify themselves.

They would not give their names, but said, "We mean you no harm. Our master sent us to bring you to meet him."

With little choice but to accept the pair's demand, the stranger accompanied them into the woods, where he came before Robin.

"Do you have any money to spare for we poor men of the forest?" the outlaw leader asked courteously. "Only five shillings," the stranger replied, "and the ring that I have kept these seven years, for my wedding day." Robin wondered when that date was to be, and the man replied, "Yesterday was to have been the day when I married my lovely maid." This explained the singing and dancing of the previous day, Robin realized. So why was the man too sad today? "She has been taken from me by the Bishop," he said, "and promised

Robin Hood interrupts a wedding in order to help Allan-a-Dale in this drawing by Howard Pyle.

to an old knight instead." Robin asked the name of the broken-hearted young man, to which he answered, "Allan-a-Dale."

Robin thought for a moment before asking, "What would Allan-a-Dale give to get his true love back?"

"I have no money to give, but I promise to be Robin Hood's true servant if he will help me."

Robin asked him how far it was to the church, and when Allan-a-Dale replied that it was five miles away, Robin knew he would have to act quickly. He was determined to save Allan-a-Dale's bride from her fate and gain a new member of the Merry Men in the bargain. Snatching up his weapons, Robin bolted from the meeting place and ran full-tilt, sprinting across the fields and stopping for nothing and no one.

When Robin Hood burst into the church, the Bishop, who was getting ready to officiate the wedding, demanded to know who he was to interrupt the Bishop's work. Robin replied that he was the best harpist in the whole of the North Country and had come to play at the wedding. That pleased the Bishop greatly, but Robin said he could not possibly begin to play until he saw the bride and bridegroom on their happy day.

Just then, the doors opened and in walked a wealthy old knight. Behind him followed a beautiful young woman with hair that shone like gold. Robin looked the couple up and down, and then made his pronouncement.

"This couple could scarcely be called a fit match. The bride should make her own choice for a husband." Robin darted to the door, took out his horn, and blew three blasts. This brought to him two-dozen bowmen at the run, with Allan-a-Dale at their head. They had followed Robin's course across the fields.

While the bowmen held the Bishop's retinue and the knight's retinue at arrow-point, Robin pointed to the bride.

"This maid chose Allan-a-Dale for her husband, and they will be married before anyone departs this church."

"The woman and Allan-a-Dale have not gone through the proper process to be married," the Bishop protested. "Church law says they were supposed to ask three times in church if anyone has any objections to their matrimony. They have not done so."

Unimpressed with the cleric's officiousness, Robin Hood pulled off the Bishop's cloak and placed it around Little John's shoulders.

"What has our new Bishop to say to that?" he asked.

The big man then marched round the church and asked seven times for objections, much to the amusement of the congregation. Little John then asked who would give away the maid to be married. Robin stepped forward to announce that he would, and added that any man who tried to take her from Allan-a-Dale would answer to him.

The wedding was a joyous affair for all concerned, with the exceptions of the humiliated Bishop and the jilted old knight. When the ceremony had concluded, the unusual wedding party disappeared into the forest, for a woodland honeymoon.

According to local folklore, the massive, Major Oak in the heart of Sherwood Forest was the site of Robin Hood and the Merry Men's main encampment. (PD)

Robin Hood's Golden Prize

Robin Hood's legendary trickery was in full force on the day he dressed as a friar and set off into the forest to have some fun with the clergy. Leaving nothing about his disguise to chance, Robin dressed in a full clerical gown, complete with hood, prayer beads and crucifix.

After strolling for a couple of miles, Robin saw two priests approaching and decided to greet them as a fellow man of the cloth. When he hailed the unsuspecting priests, he told them that he had been wandering all day but could not find anything to eat or even get a drink.

"Could my fellow brothers in the cloth spare me a silver groat," he asked, "in the name of the Virgin Mary?"

The two priests claimed hurriedly that they had no money, because the notorious outlaw Robin Hood had robbed them that very morning.

The notorious outlaw, who had certainly not yet robbed anyone this day, now revealed himself to the astonished priests and called them liars. The two clerics immediately turned and ran, but Robin was quickly on their heels and soon caught up to them. Grabbing them by their hoods, he dragged them to the ground. The two priests cowered from his wrath, and begged Robin to spare them.

"You did just tell me you had no money with which to buy my favor," the outlaw reminded them. "The best thing you can do would be to pray for some to turn up, and soon."

The priests immediately knelt and prayed loudly to God to send them some money.

ROBIN AND FRIAR TUCK (OPPOSITE)

Robin sets out with a few companions to seek out the curtal Friar – one who wears his robes tucked into his belt – perhaps his name refers to this. Robin goes forward alone to meet him at "Fountains Abbey" that Howard Pyle explains isn't the big one in Yorkshire, but a much smaller one in Sherwood Forest. There is indeed still an area in Sherwood that the locals call Fountain Dale, although how Pyle could have known this in his home of Wilmington, Delaware is just another part of his mystique.

The jovial episode of Robin and Tuck carrying each other across the stream is often illustrated in treatments for children, but the tale takes a darker turn when, during the sword-fight that ensues, the Friar whistles up his pack of hunting dogs. Pyle has him do this in response to Robin calling his companions with his horn, but earlier tales make them seem more like the fighting dogs of yore. They are, in any case, a part of Tuck's armory and Robin, as usual, has to beat a hasty retreat.

Tuck, one of the very few clerical characters in the tales who is not grasping and corrupt, famously joins the outlaw band, presumably dogs and all. They seem to have been dropped from later filmic treatments where Tuck loses his fierce edge and often becomes the comedy relief of the Merry Men.

- Peter Dennis

Robin sang little songs to himself while he watched the men praying, but after an hour he ended the charade, having grown bored with it.

"Shall we see what money God has sent in answer to your prayers?" he suggested.

He ordered the priests to search through their clothes and place down on the ground anything they found.

"We shall share fairly anything that God had sent," Robin promised. The priests did as they were instructed and searched themselves, but produced no money. Annoyed at their continued dissembling, Robin roughly searched both priests. He found coin after coin until 500 gold pieces lay on the grass at their feet.

Robin was delighted.

"Thanks to your most excellent prayers," he said, "God has provided, and so you may each take one share of the gold." Robin gave both of them 50 pounds, but the priests could only sigh at their overall misfortune. The two chastened clerics backed away and turned to leave, but Robin was not quite finished with them. He made them swear three oaths before he allowed them to go on their way. The first oath was that they would never tell lies again; the second was that they would never tempt young women to sin, and nor would they cheat on husbands with their wives; finally, they were to take an oath to be charitable to the poor, and that they were to tell anyone who asked that they met with a true holy friar.

Having administered his lesson to the priests, Robin let them go about their business, while he returned into the forest, having taken care of his.

Robin Hood and Queen Catherine

Queen Catherine and the King were sitting in their garden one afternoon, when he asked if there was any entertainment she would like for him to arrange. The Queen asked for an archery competition the likes of which had never been seen and suggested that they should make a bet on the outcome. The King, amused, said he would go easy on her and would stake 300 barrels of wine, 300 barrels of beer, and 300 of his best deer that his chosen archer would win.

The Queen readily accepted this wager, because she had a plan up her sleeve. She went straight to her chambers and called for her page, Partington.

"Make ready to travel with all speed to Nottingham," she told him, "where you shall scour the countryside to find Robin Hood. When you have found him, give this ring to the outlaw, and tell him that it is safe to come to London."

She explained the bet she had made with the King and she wanted Robin Hood to represent her. Partington was soon on his way north.

Partington's first port of call in Nottingham was at an inn, where he ordered a glass of wine and offered a toast to the Queen. A yeoman sidled up and asked him his business this far north.

"I have come in search of Robin Hood," he replied.

"Robin Hood?" the yeoman echoed. "Come by tomorrow morning, and I'll see that you're taken to meet him."

Partington was up bright and early the next day and, as promised, the yeoman led him into the forest. It did not take long before they came to the outlaw stronghold, and when he was introduced to Robin Hood, Partington fell immediately to his knees. He offered the Queen's greetings and gave the outlaw leader her ring. He then asked Robin if he would travel to London to represent the Queen in the archery contest.

In reply, Robin gave the page his cloak of Lincoln green.

"Take this to the Queen as my token of acceptance."

He then added that if he lost the contest, he would pay the Queen's losses himself.

Robin Hood next had to decide which of his Merry Men would accompany him to London for the contest and who would stay behind. Little John was Robin's first choice, of course, and then Much the Miller's Son, and Will Scarlett. Soon, Robin and his small entourage left for London, suitably attired for their Royal duty. Robin had dressed himself in scarlet, and his party of men in Lincoln green. All of them wore black hats with white feathers and carried yew bows with silk strings and engraved arrows.

When Robin and his band reached London, the Queen personally welcomed him to the city, with the words "Greetings to my Lord of Loxley," in order to

A painting by N.C. Wyeth of the first meeting between Robin Hood and Maid Marian. In later versions of the stories, Marian often takes the place of the Queen at the archery tournament. (PARIS PIERCE / Alamy)

keep his true identity a secret. The Queen then went to speak to the King in his private chambers. She confessed to him that she had been unable to find a single archer in her Royal court that would accept the challenge to shoot against the King's men.

The King nodded, acknowledging that, "My archers are the best in England. Only Robin Hood could even hope to compete with them."

The Queen, enjoying his unknowing irony, promptly doubled her bet against the over-confident King.

The Royal party then made their way to Finsbury, where the competition would be held.

When they arrived at Finsbury, the King called over a man named Tempest.

"This shall be my champion archer," he told the Queen. "There is no finer archer in the service of England, Spain, or France," he boasted.

The Queen responded by presenting her champion.

"This is Loxley."

She tapped her archer three times on the head, and warned, "Pay heed because this man is just as good as your champion."

Tensions between the competitors rose immediately when the King ordered Tempest to measure out the distance at which he wanted to shoot.

At this point, Robin stepped boldly forward to claim that, "No measures will be necessary, your Grace, because we will shoot at the sun and the moon." At that, Little John broke into the bragging to suggest a distance of 300 yards. That was agreeable to all and the archers prepared for the competition.

In the first round, Robin Hood, Little John, and Much all let fly at their targets, but the King's archers beat them on every shot, immediately taking a three to nil lead. The ladies-in-waiting cried to their Queen that the contest was lost, but the Queen remained remarkably confident. She asked the King if two of his privy councillors might want to lay a bet for her team. The King looked round for two volunteers, granting permission for them to bet with his Queen. The Queen called upon Sir Richard of the Lea who she knew to be a good knight and descended from the knights of Arthur's Round Table. He, of course, was also a good friend to Robin Hood, though he hadn't recognized the outlaw in his disguise as Loxley.

The Queen also called for the Bishop of Hereford to bet on her side, but he would have none of it.

The Bishop scoffed, and said, "I would not bet a single penny on a bunch of unknown archers from the north against the King's finest."

Overhearing this, Robin approached the Bishop, whom he recognized as the man that he had tied to a tree and forced to say Mass for his men.

He asked, "If you won't bet on me, then what would you bet against me?"

"I will stake the entire contents of my purse," the Bishop replied. When Robin inquired just how much the Bishop carried, the cleric laid out 300 Nobles, which came to 100 pounds. Robin took the bet.

Robin and Marian by James Edwin McConnell. Maid Marian is one of the later additions to the story of Robin Hood and thus does not appear in the early legends or myths. When she does finally appear, she is originally treated equally with the other Merry Men. It is only later, in the late 19th and 20th centuries that she is softened and more often presented as a damsel in distress. (Look and Learn / The Bridgeman Art Library)

The arrows flew once more, and, after the second round, the score was tied at three apiece. "Your champions' fortunes have changed," the King remarked to the Queen, "but there are still three points to play for, and Tempest is up next."

Indeed, Tempest loosed next, a perfect shot that placed in the exact dead-center of the target. The King was delighted, and no one could see how that shot could possibly be beaten. Determined not to let the Queen down, Robin stepped up to the mark, drew the bowstring to his ear, took aim down the length of the clothyard shaft, and loosed.

The speeding arrow struck in the exact same spot as Tempest's arrow, splitting the shaft of that arrow into three pieces to get to it. After the second of the King's archers had his final shot, Little John took his, and he also split his opponent's arrow. Will Scarlett strode forward, bowed to the Queen, and then let fly – his arrow struck dead-center in the bullseye. When the shock of defeat hit Tempest, he rushed to the King.

"Your Grace, only men trained by the outlaw Robin Hood himself could have out-shot my men and I," he complained. It was now time for the Queen to reveal her surprise.

Before the Queen told the King the truth, she asked for his forgiveness in advance to be extended to any of her archers. Curious, he promised her that if they had done anything wrong, they would have 40 days to make their getaway, and then another 80 days of freedom before any attempt would be made to arrest them. Satisfied with her husband's answer, the Queen introduced her champion and his men.

"May I present Robin Hood, of Sherwood Forest, his Lieutenant, John Little, Much, and Will Scarlett."

The Bishop of Hereford was especially stunned by this revelation, because he had not recognized the outlaw who had captured him, bound him to a tree, and made him sing a Mass.

"Had I known you," the Bishop spluttered, "I would have raised the alarm, not made a bet."

"I was very pleased with your Mass," Robin said. "So pleased, in fact, you may have half my winnings from you as compensation."

Little John intervened, telling Robin Hood that they would be better served giving the money to the King's officers.

Having won the contest for the Queen, and been granted safe conduct and a period of grace by the King, the outlaws left to return to their northern forest home.

The Death of Robin Hood

For 22 years, Robin Hood lived in his beloved forest, rarely leaving for fear of the King's revenge for leaving his sworn service. It would not be the King, however, but Robin's cousin that would bring him down in the end.

Robin Hood and Little John were hunting in the woods one morning, when Robin complained of feeling weak. The solution, he decided, was to ask his cousin, who lived at nearby Kirklees Abbey, to bleed him, because that was the best way to release the evil humors from his body. When they returned to the Merry Men, and told them of Robin's decision, Will Scarlett shook his head.

"If you truly must go to Kirklees, then you should take at least 50 of our bowmen with you. Roger of Doncaster lives in that area, and he bears you ill will."

Robin would not hear of it. "I have no fear of Red Roger," he insisted, and told Scarlett that he was only going to take Little John with him to carry his bow.

The last arrow of Robin Hood as drawn by Howard Pyle.

Robin Hood arrives at Kirklees Abbey where he is greeted by a nun. In the early tales of Robin, there is no motivation given for why the nun, who is Robin's cousin, ends up killing the outlaw. (Look and Learn / The Bridgeman Art Library)

"I'll go with you," the big man agreed, "but you can carry your own bow! I shall carry mine, and we will have a shooting contest."

Robin agreed, cheered by the thought, and the two men left alone.

They had walked most of the day, and dusk was falling, when Little John and Robin came to a dark stream, bridged by a wooden plank. An old woman was kneeling on the plank, lamenting the fate of Robin Hood.

Robin asked, "What fate is there to lament of Robin Hood? Have you heard ominous reports of him?"

"I weep because Robin is to be bled this day, and I fear for him."

Robin was perplexed but reassured the old woman. "I am Robin Hood, and the Prioress of the Abbey is my cousin, and she would do me no harm."

He and Little John were soon on their way again.

When they reached the Abbey, Robin asked Little John to wait outside in the grounds, then knocked on the door. The Prioress herself came to the door, invited Robin in, and told him to make himself comfortable.

The outlaw gave her 20 pounds, promised her more if she should need it, and then explained that he was feeling weak and needed to be bled. The Prioress left to fetch her bleeding-knives, but was soon back and making Robin ready by rolling up his sleeve. She began the bleeding, and Robin's blood soon poured into a dish placed beneath his arm. The bleeding continued until Robin realized too late that he had bled too much. Realizing his danger, he knocked the dish away and tried to climb out through the window, but he was too weak. Then Robin reached for his horn and blew on it three times to call for help.

Little John heard Robin's horn-blasts, but the lack of strength in the notes worried him greatly. He ran to the Abbey's entrance and crashed through the locked doors in a shower of splintered wood. He found Robin in distress at being tricked by his cousin. Robin told Little John of the danger he was in, and, grabbing his sword, he again tried to leave by climbing out of the window. Before he could get there, however, Red Roger burst into the room and stabbed Robin in the side. Robin was not yet finished, though; he side-stepped Red Roger's next cut, before slashing a gaping wound into his neck.

The Prioress shrieked as Roger of Doncaster fell, and dropped to her knees to hold him in her arms as he expired.

"My love," she cried, and now Robin understood why she had tricked him.

Looking down at the fatally wounded man, Robin told him, "The dogs will have you for their supper. We might both be bled to death, but at least I will receive the last rites."

Knowing that he was dying, Robin turned to Little John and asked the big outlaw to administer the last rites to him.

"Let me burn down the Abbey instead," John replied. Robin shook his head.

"I have never done harm to women, and God would not forgive me if we did so now." Instead, Robin asked Little John to pass him his bow, so that he could shoot an arrow through the window.

"Wherever in the grounds this arrow lands," he said, "should be my grave. A proper grave, so that people will always remember where Robin Hood is buried, here in this Abbey."

Finally he added, "And bury my bow beside me."

Little John agreed, and, with that, Robin nocked an arrow and let it fly through the open window before slumping down, succumbing to the loss of blood from both the Prioress's bleeding, and the wound that Red Roger had given him.

Little John honored his friend's last wish and Robin Hood lies there still in the grounds of Kirklees Abbey.

Robin Hood's Death and Burial.

' Lay me a green sod under my head,
   And another at my feet ;
And lay my bent bow by my side,
   Which was my music sweet ;
And make my grave of gravel and green,
   Which is most right and meet.

' Let me have length and breadth enough,
   With a green sod under my head ;
That they may say, when I am dead,
   Here lies bold Robin Hood.'

These words they readily promis'd him,
   Which did bold Robin please :
And there they buried bold Robin Hood,
   Near to the fair Kirklèys.

Robin Hood's World

Who Was Robin Hood?

If we believe there was a historical Robin Hood, who was he? Reading the legend, it would seem that an outlaw of such fame would be easy to identify in the records. The ravages of time, however, have worn holes in the historical records, particularly those that might refer to a man of lower than noble status. Moreover, both "Robin," "Hood," and their close variants were common names in the Middle Ages, and our failure to pin down the exact dates for the outlaw increases considerably the pool of candidates. Historians have

therefore found claimants for the original Robin Hood in the reigns of kings from John, who took the throne in 1199, to Edward III, who died in 1377.

Nevertheless, a few top contenders stand out from the rest.

Hereward the Wake

The earliest, and arguably most famous, candidate for the original Robin Hood was Hereward the Wake. Hereward dates back to the years immediately following the Norman invasion of 1066, when he led a pocket of resistance from his base on the Isle of Ely, in modern-day Cambridgeshire. His most famous exploit was the pillaging of Peterborough Abbey in 1071. That event, at least, is historical, but much of what was written about Hereward's exploits, including his disguise as a potter to fool the Normans, is probably apocryphal.

The Normans captured Hereward's stronghold by treachery, and he subsequently disappears from the record; although a Hereward does appear in the Doomsday Book of 1087, suggesting some form of reconciliation or Royal pardon. It might be that, while Hereward is an unlikely candidate for Robin Hood himself, his exploits, as told in his biography *De Gestis Herewardi Saxonis*, became part of the tales attributed to the outlaw of legend.

Fulk fitzWarin

Another outlaw whose exploits undoubtedly taint the Robin Hood legend was Fulk fitzWarin. He was a Shropshire baron outlawed in 1200 for murdering a rival claimant in a property dispute. For the next three years, fitzWarin ran a bandit operation along the Welsh marches against the forces of King John. The King pardoned him in 1203, but in 1215 fitzWarin joined the Baronial Rebellion. Pardoned once more in 1217, fitzWarin lived out the rest of his life peaceably. Like Robin Hood, fitzWarin became a subject of ballads, and many of his alleged adventures became intertwined with those of the more famous outlaw.

William of Keynsham

The First Baron's War, fought between 1215 and 1217, casts up another candidate for Robin Hood. On that occasion, the barons were in dire straits and called on a French prince to displace King John and assume the throne. The French promptly invaded and established control over a wide area of England. They struggled in the Forest of Dean, however, because of the remarkable resistance led by one William of Keynsham.

William led nearly a thousand men in defying the French, killing thousands of the invaders, cutting their supply lines, and launching surprise attacks on their garrisons. William was lavishly rewarded by the King when the French were finally defeated in 1217, receiving land and money for his services. Thus, William became a heroic outlaw in charge of a band of archers, fighting against tyranny. William of Keynsham's candidacy might also help explain the concentration of records relating to the surname Hood in South East England, which is where William was most active.

Roger Godberd

The pivotal event that brings Robert Godberd to our attention as a suspect was the Battle of Evesham in 1265. He fought for the rebellious upstart Earl of Leicester, Simon de Montfort, against the forces of Henry III in the Second Barons' War. Godberd's side lost disastrously, and de Montfort died in the battle. That left men like Godberd without a leader, so he took to Sherwood Forest with up to 100 men, to continue a guerrilla war for the lost cause.

He led the local authorities a merry dance for four years before being caught and jailed in Nottingham Castle. He escaped with the help of a knight named

A hand-colored 19th century woodcut depicting Robin Hood and Little John. It is unusual in its depiction of Little John as a fully armored soldier. (North Wind Picture Archives / Alamy)

THE SHOOTING MATCH (OPPOSITE)

For the agricultural medieval Englishman, the main audience for the Robin Hood plays and ballads, archery was an important part of life. More than just a sporting pastime, it was his legal duty to spend time at the butts, shooting with his pals from the village. He might have preferred to play football, but quite often that was banned by statute as a useless distraction. When the local troops were called up, he had to be able to report in with his bow and the skill to use it.

Shooting matches, many of which feature in the tales, were a festival of marksmanship, probably with all the fun of the fair thrown in, and would draw archers from a good distance around to try for the prize.

Robin was often bested in hand-to-hand combat but never in archery, and here he is disguised, according to Pyle, as a one-eyed man in ragged scarlet.

The contest is down to two men now. His opponent has nailed his shaft to the very center of the mark, but Robin's broadhead will split it from nock to pile to the amazement of the gathering. The man in red will win the silver arrow.

Somehow, despite their frequent meetings, the Sheriff fails to see through Robin's disguise and hands over the prize to the mysterious stranger.

- *Peter Dennis*

Richard Foliot. The knight would pay for aiding the outlaw by losing his castle. Godberd went back to his outlaw ways but was recaptured and moved around to various prisons while awaiting trial. When Edward I ascended the throne, however, he pardoned Godberd, who apparently went on to live out the rest of his life as a law-abiding citizen.

Robert Hode of Wakefield

Robert Hode of Wakefield appears a century after William of Keynsham. He became a leading suspect when his name was uncovered in relation to the northern progress of Edward II in 1323. Like Roger Godberd, Robert Hode took up the outlaw life after being on the wrong side of a rebellion, and subsequent military defeat, this time at Boroughbridge in 1322. This was a time of considerable banditry in the north, and other candidates of that time have emerged to make their case as being the origin of the Robin Hood legend.

What makes Robert Hode different is that he appears in the records as a servant of the King in 1324, and earlier, in 1316, when he was summoned to fight for the Royal army under Earl Thomas of Lancaster, who led the 1322 rebellion. Thus it is claimed that Edward II must have pardoned Robert Hode, for him to enter the King's service. If the records alluded to the same man then that would fit neatly with the legend and make Robert Hode a strong candidate.

The Best of the Rest

Other candidates for the original Robin Hood abound, but, as befits men of the forest, we catch only glimpses of them in the records.

Alexander Robehood was a wanted man in Essex in 1272, while in that same year John Rabunhood fled from a murder charge in Hampshire. Robert

Robehood was another Hampshire criminal of the late 13th century. Thirty years earlier a William Robehod plied his outlaw trade in Berkshire, though that was not his real name. Potential Robin Hoods are found even earlier in the 1200s, at Cirencester, and in County Durham.

The Sheriff of York hunted a Robert of Wetherby in 1225, but he, like the rest of our suspects, remains elusive when it comes to finding that actual evidence to mark him as the Robin Hood of legend and myth.

When Was Robin Hood?

One of the reasons why the Robin Hood legend endures so well is the lack of specific references as to when he lived. It is timeless.

There are no records of a real Robin Hood that match the description of the famous outlaw, nor do we know of a Little John, Will Scarlett, Much the Miller's Son, or any of the Merry Men. Even the Sheriff of Nottingham is known only by his title. In fact, there is not a single person in any of the ballads constituting the original legends that historians can place with anything approaching certainty.

We are left, then, with an exciting medieval fable, but the suspicion remains that there was a real outlaw behind the legend, and that it might be easier to trace his identity if only we knew for sure when he existed.

The first definite reference we have for Robin Hood is a throwaway remark in William Langland's *Piers Plowman*, written in 1377. It is fair to surmise that the legend of Robin Hood was widely enough circulated by then to make the reference meaningful. The earliest surviving ballads, however, originate from the 15th century; therefore contamination of the oral record had had plenty of time to seep into the text. As time passed, more ballads surfaced, with new details, but tracing them back to the origins of the Robin Hood story becomes ever more difficult. Placing Robin Hood into a specific chronology is, therefore, extraordinarily difficult.

The first attempts to fix Robin in history came in the early 15th century, with two Scottish writers who placed him between 1266 and 1285. A little later the first reference was posited to the reign of Richard the Lionheart, with whom Robin is popularly associated.

In the 17th century, antiquarians used a seemingly still-extant grave slab at Kirklees Priory (thought to be the Kirklees Abbey of the stories) to date Robin's death as either 1247, or 1198, but the slab is now lost, and modern historians frown upon such things as lack of evidence. Writing in 1852, Joseph Hunter calculated – on the basis of a single Royal progress, and recorded names in Court Rolls – that Robin was active in the 1320s. Hunter's date has proved popular, but there is again no evidence to connect the names he found to an outlaw of a similar name, and coincidence is not enough to convict.

A century after Hunter, historian J. W. Walker promoted the 1320s connection by determining that the Robert Hood of Wakefield found in contemporary army rolls was the famous outlaw, but Walker, too, relied on coincidence and stretching the evidence to cover obvious gaps in the record. The 14th century connection is bolstered by the mention in one ballad of King Edward, putting the outlaw firmly in the period of the three kings of that name, somewhere between 1272 and 1377. The King's name may be a later addition, however, and there is evidence to show that the legend was already known in 1261. That has led one modern historian, Sean McGlynn, to place the "inspiration" for Robin Hood in the early 13th century, in the guise of an English freedom fighter against a French invasion.

Another historian, Rupert Matthews, argues that Robin was quite possibly an actual outlaw operating sometime in the middle

Plaque marking the supposed site of the burial of Robin Hood. (David Speight / Alamy)

SPONSORED BY MIRFIELD TOWN COUNCIL

THE THREE NUNS

A TAVERN PROBABLY STOOD ON THIS SITE IN THE 16TH C. AND MAYBE AS LONG AGO AS THE 14TH C. KIRKLEES PRIORY LAY WITHIN THE GROUNDS OF KIRKLEES PARK BEHIND THE THREE NUNS AND IN THE SAME GROUNDS IS THE GRAVE OF ROBIN HOOD. FOLLOWING THE DISSOLUTION OF THE MONASTERIES IN 1539 BY HENRY VIII THREE NUNS FROM THE PRIORY MAY HAVE TAKEN OVER THE TAVERN. IN 1565 THE ARMYTAGE FAMILY BOUGHT THE KIRKLEES ESTATE INCLUDING THE INN AND OWNED IT UNTIL 1935 WHEN IT WAS SOLD TO RAMSDEN'S BREWERY. THE PRESENT BUILDING WAS BUILT IN 1939.

MIRFIELD CIVIC SOCIETY

Robin Hood's Bay, North Yorkshire in the late 19th century. According to an old legend, French pirates attacked the village and made off with all of its treasure. Later, Robin Hood captured the pirates and returned the stolen wealth. The village changed its name in a show of thanks. (Library of Congress)

of the 13th century. What the latter two attempts to pin the tail on the donkey demonstrate is that the Robin Hood legend obviously eludes easy chronological dating, and that the approach to identifying the original Robin Hood is essentially blocked off by the lack of historically measurable detail.

Where Was Robin Hood?

Robin Hood is most commonly associated with Sherwood Forest, particularly near the town of Nottingham in north-central England. On the face of it, that territory makes sense because it is, after all, the Sheriff of Nottingham who attempts – and fails – so often to capture the outlaw, so it's logical Robin must fall within his jurisdiction. In addition, many place names in and around Sherwood Forest are associated with the legend. A careful reading of the Robin Hood ballads shows, however, that his connection to Nottinghamshire is not quite as secure as it might seem.

Much of the speculation on where Robin Hood conducted his outlaw activities depends upon which camp the analyst falls within with regard to discussing his identity. As we have seen, that consideration casts a wide net. Nevertheless, certain places reoccur in the Robin Hood ballads that firmly locate him in a broad triangle with its corners at Nottingham, Warrington, and Wakefield. Barnesdale, for example, mentioned in more than one ballad, lies just to the east of the Nottingham–Wakefield road, in the environs of Doncaster. Kirklees Priory, where Robin Hood met his end, sits northwest of Wakefield.

The most common place directly associated with Robin Hood's name is Loxley, or Locksley – as in Robin of Loxley – which is commonly associated with an ancient plot of land in the Sheffield area, directly along the Nottingham–Wakefield road. Moreover, the Sheriff's jurisdiction was not just in Nottingham, but spread over towards the nearby town of Derby, and up into South Yorkshire.

Maybe, then, when looking for Robin Hood, we might bump into him disguised as a potter or monk in a small town or village, avoiding the Sheriff of Nottingham, or we might catch glimpses of him flitting among the trees in Sherwood Forest, but we should also not be surprised if we are waylaid by a familiar looking outlaw almost anywhere along the highways or byways leading north or west out of Nottingham.

According to local legend, Little John was born and died in the village of Hathersage in Derbyshire. His gravestone can be seen in the yard of St. Michael's church. (© Alan Copson/JAI/ Corbis)

The Merry Men

The endurance of the Robin Hood myth relies not just on the exploits of the legendary outlaw himself, but also on the remarkable cast of characters that formed his band. Fully assembled, the Merry Men formed an illustrious company, worthy of any great adventure; the strong man, the bard, the trickster, the youthful acolyte, and the romantic love-interest. Yet the Robin Hood of legend might have been quite surprised at some of the people with whom he later became associated.

Little John

The ironically named Little John was Robin Hood's most trusted companion. Where he came from, we do not know, but he appears in the earliest stories of Robin Hood and is with him at his death. They meet in the myth when Little John stops Robin from crossing a stream in the forest. Robin loses the subsequent fight, but Little John agrees to join Robin's band anyway. When he is introduced to the rest of Robin's Merry Men, one of them changes the name of the hulking seven-foot tall man from John Little into Little John. However, there is no origin story for how the two men met in the original legend.

HERE LIES BURIED
LITTLE JOHN
THE FRIEND & LIEUTENANT OF
ROBIN HOOD
HE DIED IN A COTTAGE (NOW DESTROYED)
TO THE EAST OF THE CHURCHYARD
THE GRAVE IS MARKED BY
THIS OLD HEADSTONE & FOOTSTONE
AND IS UNDERNEATH THIS OLD YEW TREE

THE DEATH OF ROBIN HOOD (OPPOSITE)

There are many versions of how Robin came to die in Kirklees Abbey. All blame the treachery of the Prioress who, despite being Robin's cousin, in the guise of helping the fevered outlaw, hastens his end.

One of the tales has her bleed him into a specially prepared dish, which in turn drains into a larger vessel, thus disguising how much blood has been taken. In others she poisons him. Pyle has her exclude Little John from the abbey while she bleeds him almost to death. Robin manages to alert his trusty companion by feebly blowing his horn. John breaks down the abbey door and joins him for the scene depicted here. Robin summons his last reserves of strength to shoot an arrow out of the window and makes John promise to bury him where the arrow falls.

- Peter Dennis

After the fight, Robin and Little John share in many adventures, though their relationship sometimes becomes very strained, and it is the big man who often comes to Robin's rescue. Indeed, on one occasion, Robin offers Little John the leadership of the outlaw band, but the loyal lieutenant refuses.

When Robin is tricked at Kirklees Abbey and lies dying, it is Little John who is the only Merry Man present, and who administers the last rites.

Little John is still an essential character in modern versions of the story, but his pivotal role in the legend has diminished as other Merry Men have come increasingly to the fore and been given more prominent places in the myth. Perennial sidekick Alan Hale Sr. played Little John three times in movies, from 1922 to 1950, and his portrayal established the character as Robin's loyal lieutenant. More modern versions, however, have been a bit more ambivalent, giving Little John more of his own personality than that assumed by Hale.

Historically, the name John Little associated with relevant outlaw activity has proven extraordinarily difficult to find. However, his burial site is allegedly in Hathersage in Derbyshire.

Will Scarlett

Will Scarlett also appears in the earliest Robin Hood ballads, though he is sometimes given the surname Scathelocke or Scarlock. Will is further down the leadership ladder in the Merry Men, but still takes on an advisory role, as well as actively engaging in their outlaw activities. He is instrumental in capturing Richard of the Lea, for example, and advises Robin to take more men than Little John to his fateful rendezvous at Kirklees Abbey.

When Robin enters the King's service, Will stays with him, along with Little John, though the rest of their group have already left to go back to their outlaw ways. As with his introduction to Little John, Robin meets Will in the forest, and they end up fighting before becoming friends. We also learn from their first encounter that Will is a fugitive from a murder charge and so is compelled to live the outlaw life.

While Will Scarlett emerges from the background less often in the legend, he is a much more developed character in the modern myth and rivals Little John as the Merry Men's surrogate leader.

A William Schirelock appears in the historical record for 1286–87, which would be around the right time and place but, as always, the links in the record have proved too elusive to firmly attach this man to the legendary outlaw.

Much the Miller's Son

Much the Miller's Son is the third identifiable outlaw from the legend stories. Much is small in stature but a skilled and ruthless fighter, who accompanies Little John on his various missions for Robin Hood. He is also one of Robin's hand-picked archers for the famous archery contest. When Robin is captured, Much volunteers to go with Little John to rescue their leader. Along the way, he commits one of the most violent acts of the legend when he decapitates the Monk's pageboy. After killing some of the Sheriff's men, Much and Little John daringly release Robin from his jail cell.

Although Much is Robin's best friend in the movie *Robin Hood: Prince of Thieves*, and is almost always involved in Robin's legendary adventures, his character has taken something of a back seat in the modern renditions. That might be because of his youth and his connection to the brutality of the decapitation of the page. However, Much's central role in Adam Thorpe's 2009 novel *Hodd* may yet move Much back to center stage in future mythmaking.

Friar Tuck

The legend often speaks of Robin Hood as dutiful when it comes to religion, even while he punished corrupt clergymen. For Robin to have as a member of his band a man who was expelled from his religious order might, therefore, make sense. Yet the legend makes no mention of Friar Tuck.

It is quite likely that Friar Tuck entered the myth through the May Games that became associated with the Robin Hood legend. The corpulent and good-humored friar has provided comic relief to offset the darker side of the Robin Hood adventures ever since, most notably when played by Eugene Pallette in *The Adventures of Robin Hood*. Pallette set the tone for future portrayals, so that in the 1950s Porky Pig became a recognizable animated substitute for the friar, though Walt Disney's use of a badger in the 1973 animated film seems a little more questionable.

Tuck enters the modern story by various means. He is a confessor to Maid Marian in some versions, echoing his connection to her in the historical May Games, while in one adaptation he is a seller of phoney relics, and in another saves Robin's life.

The earliest printed version of the story relating Robin's encounter with Friar Tuck at the river crossing dates to the 17th century. If we accept a friar as

one of Robin Hood's retinue, though, then the outlaw cannot be dated before 1224, when friars first landed in England.

That would rule out any of the associations between Robin Hood, King John, and Richard the Lionheart that have appeared in the myth almost ubiquitously since the 19th century. Some historians have noted a renegade monk of the early 15th century who bears a similar name to Friar Tuck, but he is clearly too late to have direct involvement with an original Robin Hood – though at the right time to have his name added to the tales.

Allan-a-Dale

Joining Friar Tuck as a latecomer to Robin Hood mythology, Allan-a-Dale complements the friar's comedy with music. A ballad dating to the 17th century has Robin meet Allan-a-Dale in the forest. The outlaw listens to the man's tale of woe and then helps rescue his fiancée from the clutches of a bishop who is about to marry her off to an old knight. Allan is so grateful that he agrees to join Robin's Merry Men.

Allan-a-Dale reappears in Howard Pyle's 1883 illustrated novel of the Robin Hood legend, *The Merry Adventures of Robin Hood*. Pyle gives him an origin story and connects him inextricably to Friar Tuck, who is the only clergyman who will defy the Bishop by marrying Allan-a-Dale to his sweetheart.

The cast of *Robin of Sherwood* which ran from 1984-86 on British television. The show brought a large dose of fantasy to the Robin Hood tales as well as being the first to introduce a Saracen to the Merry Men. The show featured Ray Winstone in the role of Will Scarlett. (Ronald Grant Archive / Mary Evans)

The young musician has become something of a staple Merry Man character in the television and film era. He is portrayed by legendary crooner Bing Crosby in the curious modernized 1964 version of the Robin Hood story set in gangster-era Chicago, *Robin and the 7 Hoods*, and is the rooster-narrator for Disney's 1973 animated rendition. The marriage story is retold in *Robin of Sherwood*, but when the BBC made its new version in 2006, Allan-a-Dale was portrayed as a treacherous petty thief with no musical ability. His good character, however, and some of his talent, is restored in Ridley Scott's 2010 movie *Robin Hood*.

Maid Marian

Of all the characters associated with Robin Hood none was less likely to be in his entourage than Maid Marian. Indeed, no women affiliated with Robin Hood's outlaw activities appear in the legend stories at all.

Like Friar Tuck, Marian likely enters the myth through the May Games festivals that became increasingly popular from the 15th century onwards. She was also probably an import from French tradition. Marian was connected directly with Robin Hood only in the 16th century, but is best remembered from the 17th century ballad bearing her name. In that story, she is a fighter capable of holding her own against Robin, but by the Victorian era, when women were expected to play more passive roles, Marian becomes more innocent and in need of Robin Hood's protection. That attitude was revived in Hollywood movies, particularly in the wake of the acceptance of the Hays Code in 1930, which locked the movie industry into a moral straitjacket. Marian's new virtuous womanhood, as displayed by Olivia de Havilland in *The Adventures of Robin Hood*, again sets the tone for future representations.

In the new millennium, Marian has been given more dynamic capabilities, befitting more enlightened attitudes, but her noble class status remains intact.

The Saracen

The introduction of a Saracen into the myth is an entirely modern phenomenon. He first appeared as Nasir in the television series *Robin of Sherwood*, which ran from 1984 to 1986. The Saracen character also plays a role in *Robin Hood: Prince of Thieves*, and the BBC series *Robin Hood*. When Ridley Scott came to make his version of the myth in 2010, however, the Saracen character was not included.

Robin Hood's Enemies

Despite being a notorious outlaw whose criminal career lasted over two decades, Robin Hood had surprisingly few enemies, although those he did have hated him very much. Moreover, while we have a name for one of Robin's enemies, and titles for two more, positive historical identification remains elusive, and the historian is left wondering if they are merely archetypes for various medieval institutions in which corruption was rife, i.e. local authorities and the Church.

The Sheriff of Nottingham

Robin Hood's main adversary is the Sheriff of Nottingham. The Sheriff was tasked with upholding the King's law in Sherwood Forest and that included arresting any outlaws disturbing the peace, molesting travellers, or poaching. It is difficult to fault the Sheriff for lack of effort when he is seemingly in endless pursuit of Robin or formulating new schemes to trap him.

On one occasion, he does capture the outlaw, but his security measures for his captive fail, and Robin escapes. Also, while Robin regularly makes a fool of the Sheriff, he never stands up to the Sheriff and his men in a fair fight, although there is no reason other than the demands of honor as to why he should. Ultimately, the Sheriff is just doing his job and will stop at nothing to end Robin's reign in Sherwood Forest, even resorting to sending a bounty hunter to kill the outlaw.

The Sheriff of Nottingham has been portrayed in various ways – as coward, fool, schemer, sociopath, opportunist, cynic, and even a literal wolf – but he is always corrupt. Walt Disney's animal stereotype for the Sheriff was a buffoonish and fat wolf, while, at the other end of the scale, Robert Shaw's 1976 depiction in *Robin and Marian* is a more sympathetic portrait of a strong-willed, ambitious official, undertaking a difficult task. Ambition also features heavily in Alan Rickman's venal Sheriff in *Robin Hood: Prince of Thieves*, who covets the throne of England.

Most modern depictions of the Sheriff, however, stick to exploiting their own jurisdiction in and around Nottingham – including Sherwood Forest – and the characterization focuses more on their corrupt methods than any broader schemes they intend to hatch.

Historians have tried to pin down the original Sheriff in their attempt to "capture" Robin Hood. The first problem is that he is never named in the legend or myth, and therefore the field of candidates is almost wide open. In addition, the first true Sheriff of Nottingham did not exist before the creation of the office in the mid-15th century, which is obviously long after the legend was born.

Moreover, Robin kills one Sheriff in the legend and Little John another, so history requires at least three sheriffs. Nevertheless, historians have found a few candidates that might fit the bill, though that is hardly surprising given the corruption in local politics, and the major political upheavals of the

In many modern myths, Robin Hood is turned into a freedom fighter against Norman oppression. In these stories, it is common for King (or Prince) John to either take the place of, or to oversee, the Sheriff of Nottingham. (PD)

13th and 14th centuries. Another option of course is that, like Robin Hood himself, the Sheriff of Nottingham may be a composite character derived from many stories about many sheriffs.

Guy of Gisborne

The bounty hunter the Sheriff hires is Guy of Gisborne. In the ballad bearing his name, Gisborne waits for Robin in the woods while wearing a grotesque horsehide. He is also well armed and almost a match for Robin when they engage in a protracted swordfight. Robin kills Gisborne and uses the bounty hunter's head to fool the Sheriff and free his comrade Little John.

Despite his small cameo in the legend, Gisborne is given a prominent role in later versions of the story. Like the Sheriff of Nottingham and the Bishop of Hereford, so little information is given in the original legend, and so little is known about any historical Guy of Gisborne, that Gisborne's character is open to wide interpretation. Indeed, it is Gisborne, not the Sheriff, who becomes the arch-villain in some modern screen mythmaking, as so brilliantly demonstrated by Basil Rathbone in *The Adventures of Robin Hood*.

Some elements of Gisborne's character are standard, such as his cruelty and brutality, and he presents a formidable foe for Robin Hood when they inevitably duel.

The Bishop of Hereford

In both the legend and myth, Robin Hood displays nothing but contempt for corrupt clergymen. He has no problem robbing passing monks, and the higher-ranked bishops present few obstacles to the clever outlaw. This antipathy is mutual, as seen in the various ballads in which Robin encounters a bishop and in particular the Bishop of Hereford. The latter is given his own ballad, dating from the 17th century, but that may have been built on previous ballads where the Bishop is unidentified even though the plot is similar.

In modern interpretations, only in the movie *Robin Hood: Prince of Thieves* is the Bishop of Hereford a named character. That may be because he is simply the representative of a corrupt Church, and therefore any Bishop will do to drive the story. Moreover, Robin Hood's other adversaries, the Sheriff of Nottingham and Guy of Gisborne, are more readily identifiable to modern audiences than a corrupt Church official, whose malfeasance might be more difficult to explain.

Historically, like the Sheriff of Nottingham, it is unclear who the character of the Bishop is based upon.

Other Enemies

In the end, it would not be the Sheriff of Nottingham, Guy of Gisborne, or the Bishop of Hereford who would kill Robin Hood, but a woman he trusts, the Prioress of Kirklees. She is Robin's cousin and bleeds him to death when he goes to her for treatment. By then, Robin has been a career criminal for over 20 years, and his instinct for preservation may finally have diminished.

The Prioress is aided by Red Roger, or Roger of Doncaster, about whom we know nothing other than those names and who appears nowhere else in either the legend or myth – though Robin's villainous cousin Roger de Courtenay in the Hammer film version, *A Challenge for Robin Hood*, may derive from this tale. The other ecclesiastical enemy of Robin Hood is the Abbot of St. Mary's, whose plot to steal Sir Richard at the Lee's land is foiled by the intervention of Robin. However, the Abbot is more of a victim of Robin's rather than an active enemy, for we hear of no retaliatory measures taken by him.

Modern mythmaking has stuck mostly to the characters contained between the legend and the myth, and therefore Robin's enemies are those we have already met. With the introduction of fantasy elements, however, and the greater liberties taken with the story in the latest versions, new antagonists have begun to emerge for Robin to overcome. In the groundbreaking *Robin of Sherwood*, the Baron Simon de Belleme uses the dark arts to control Little John, until Robin kills the sorcerous Baron. He is followed by Lord Owen of Clune, a pagan sorcerer who continues Belleme's fight.

In Robin Hood: Prince of Thieves, it is the witch Mortianna that adds the fantasy element, while in the BBC's 2006 version of Robin Hood, Guy of Gisborne is given a sister, Isabella, who becomes a foe of Robin and his Merry Men. Ridley Scott's Robin Hood introduced Sir Godfrey, a knight with dynastic ambitions loosely based on the character of Guy of Gisborne.

Robin Hood and the Merry Men as painted by the famous American illustrator N.C. Wyeth. Wyeth was a pupil of Howard Pyle. (Look and Learn / The Bridgeman Art Library)

ROBIN HOOD: THE MODERN MYTH

The legend and myth of Robin Hood continues to play well with audiences in the age of mass entertainment. Indeed, his story was one of the first told by the embryonic film industry before World War I, with the release of two silent movie versions. The third silent version in 1922, starring major film star Douglas Fairbanks Sr., brought Robin Hood's story to mass prominence, but it was the colorful blockbuster *The Adventures of Robin Hood*, starring the pre-eminent swashbuckler, Errol Flynn, that sealed the worldwide popularity of Robin Hood that endures to this day.

After World War II, Robin's story continued to be told on the big screen, most notably in Disney's 1952 movie *The Story of Robin Hood and His Merrie Men*, before making the leap to television in 1953 through a short-lived BBC series starring Patrick Troughton as the famous outlaw. That was followed by a longer-running series in Britain from 1955 to 1960. The Robin Hood myth spread by the medium of film to Germany and Italy in the 1960s and then on to Japan and the Soviet Union in later incarnations.

In 1967, Robin Hood became a space myth in *Rocket Robin Hood*, and six years later Walt Disney transformed him into a wily cartoon fox. The 1970s also saw the first comedic Robin Hoods, in *Up the Chastity Belt* and *When Things Were Rotten*, but the adventure also turned much darker in *Robin and Marian*, starring Sean Connery and Audrey Hepburn as an aging version of the mythical couple.

The growing popularity of the fantasy genre breathed new life into the Robin Hood myth in the 1980s. The standard-bearer for this new approach was the television series *Robin of Sherwood*, which ran on British TV from 1984 to 1986. This version began with an origin story for Robin of Loxley, who is persuaded by a mystic huntsman to fight the Normans from his base in Sherwood Forest. The main antagonist is still the Sheriff of Nottingham,

Douglas Fairbanks Sr. as Robin Hood and Enid Bennett as Maid Marian from the 1922 silent film *Robin Hood*.

but the bounty hunter Guy of Gisborne is now the Sheriff's deputy. In an innovative twist, Robin of Loxley is killed halfway through the series, and a young nobleman, Robert of Huntingdon, joins the fight, thereby reconciling a contradiction contained in the legend and myth over the social class background of Robin Hood.

Robin of Sherwood also introduces a completely new character in the form of a Saracen, Nasir, who is a prisoner brought back from the Crusade and released by Robin Hood. Magic and allusions to pre-Christian mysticism abound throughout the series aided by the haunting soundtrack composed by Clannad.

Many of these elements of *Robin of Sherwood* found their way into Kevin Costner's *Robin Hood: Prince of Thieves* in 1991. Of particular note is Morgan Freeman's portrayal of the Saracen, now named Azeem. He returns with Robin Hood from Jerusalem, where Robin had been held prisoner. In this version, Marian is the sister of Robin's friend who died while escaping the prison with Robin. On his arrival home, Robin finds his pre-Crusade life in tatters and takes to the forest with Azeem to fight against the evil Sheriff of Nottingham, who runs the country in the King's absence. Guy of Gisborne is now the Sheriff's cousin, and the corrupt Bishop of Hereford plays a larger role than in other versions of the myth. The fantasy element from the stories is furthered by the introduction of a witch, Mortianna, who comes close to killing Robin but is foiled by Azeem. Of the Merry Men, Will Scarlett is given a greater role than in the traditional stories and, in fact, is revealed as Robin's half-brother. Also, Friar Tuck joins the Merry Men after his capture by Robin, though his control over 50 hunting dogs as in the original Friar Tuck myth is forgotten. In the end, after a series of adventures as befits the myth, Robin marries Marian, and the King, played by Sean Connery, returns to pardon Robin.

The popularity of *Robin Hood: Prince of Thieves* did not lead to a flourishing of the Robin Hood myth, and it would be over another decade before another major attempt was made to regenerate the legend. In 2006, however, the British Broadcasting Corporation produced a new series titled simply, *Robin Hood*. In this complicated retelling of the myth, Robin, played by Jonas Armstrong, has returned from five years of service in the Third Crusade. When he gets home to Nottingham, he finds the town under the despotic rule of the Sheriff.

Kevin Costner as Robin Hood in *Robin Hood: Prince of Thieves*. Despite a mixed critical reception, the film was a hit at the box office and became the most popular interpretation of the character for a generation. (Mary Evans)

Sean Connery and Audrey Hepburn in the 1976 film, *Robin and Marian*. In this dark retelling of the end of Robin Hood's life, Maid Marian, who has become an abbess, feeds Robin poison under the guise of tending his wounds. She then takes the poison herself, supposedly out of mercy for them both. (© Douglas Kirkland/Corbis)

Robin is soon outlawed, and that acts as the gateway to a wide-ranging series of adventures until, in the end, Robin is poisoned and killed. Much is Robin's best friend in this version, while Little John joins the Merry Men after working with a rival outlaw gang. Will Scarlett and Allan-a-Dale are rescued from hanging by Robin, and the by-now-customary Saracen, this time named Djaq, is a girl disguised as her brother. Guy of Gisborne returns to his status as deputy to the Sheriff of Nottingham but he now has a ruthlessly ambitious sister who in turn befriends Robin, then betrays him, in order to become the Sheriff. That leads to Gisborne reconciling with Robin, and then dying with the outlaw in the climactic final episode. Before then, however, Guy kills the Lady Marian, and Will Scarlett returns to the Holy Land with the Saracen.

In addition to taking wide-ranging liberties with the Robin Hood legend, the BBC allows its characters to wear anachronistic clothes and brandish orientalized weapons in a story of rural English outlaws, but that is also a symptom of how the essential story of Robin Hood resonates so strongly that it can contain so many differences in how it is brought to new and appreciative audiences. That would also prove true in 2010 when Robin Hood would once more receive the Hollywood blockbuster treatment.

New Zealand star Russell Crowe took on the role of Robin Hood in Ridley Scott's movie named after the legendary outlaw leader. However, rather than attempt to retell the legend, Scott opted for an imaginative prequel. The movie is set at the turn of the 12th century and once more the action takes place among soldiers returning from the Third Crusade. Crowe plays Robin Longstride who, along with his friends Allan-a-Dale, Will Scarlett, and Little John, encounters the dying Robert of Loxley and agrees to carry the man's sword home to his father in Nottingham. Robin assumes the dying man's identity and continues on his way.

Once in England, Robin is persuaded to maintain his disguise by the dead Loxley's father, and his widow, Marian. In the meantime, Robin is being hunted by the evil Sir Godfrey, who is also rampaging across the north of England in pursuit of taxes for King John and stirring up trouble to create a baronial revolt that would result in French intervention. It is the French who are Godfrey's true paymasters.

The movie ends with the French landing near Dover but opposed by an English army in which Robin is the hero. Robin kills Godfrey in the midst of the fighting but King John is instantly envious of Robin's popularity and orders him outlawed. Robin takes refuge in Sherwood Forest with his band of Merry Men and, of course, the Lady Marian. Thus, as the movie concludes, the legend begins.

As with the other modern renditions of the Robin Hood story, Scott's movie combines history, anachronisms, legend, myth, and modern political protest to take the outlaw's story in a new direction. Moreover, the popularity of Scott's movie demonstrates that the Robin Hood myth shows no signs of retreating back into the mists of time as new productions take place for new generations.

GLOSSARY

Acolyte: Someone who assists or follows another.

Anachronism: Something or someone that belongs to a time period other than the one that it exists in.

Antipathy: A feeling of dislike that deeply rooted; a distaste for something or someone.

Apotheosis: The pinnacle, or highest point.

Archetype: A common example of a particular person or thing; a symbol that keeps returning in art, literature, or mythology.

Avaricious: Being extremely greedy for wealth; very materialistic.

Broadhead: An arrowhead that is flat, made of steel, and has very sharp edges.

Butt: A type of backstop, such as a bank or mound, that catches arrows when they are shot at a target.

Coalesce: To come together to form a whole.

Curtal: Wearing a short frock, as in the curtal monk.

Diminutive: Very small.

Ecclesiastical: Relating to clergy or to the Church.

Groat: A kind of English coin that was used during the 13th–17th centuries.

Hypocrisy: False virtue; the practice of claiming to have moral beliefs but behaving as though one doesn't have them.

Impecunious: Not having money, or very little of it; being penniless.

Impunity: Exclusion from punishment or freedom from the harmful consequences of an action.

Itinerant: Someone who wanders from one place to another.

Lincoln green: A kind of woolen fabric that is a bright green in color and that was once made in Lincoln, England, and worn by the foresters who officially watched Royal forests in Great Britain.

Malfeasance: Misconduct, especially by a public official.

Pinder: Also called a poundmaster, or one who impounds stray animals.

Portent: A forewarning or sign that something evil is about to happen.

Temporal: Relating to secular or worldly matters as opposed to spiritual ones.

Ubiquitous: Appearing or existing everywhere.

Yeoman: Someone who farms his own property.

For More Information

Experience Nottinghamshire
Nottingham Tourism Center
Website: http://www.experiencenottinghamshire.com
This center is the official organization for promoting tourism in Nottinghamshire in
    the United Kingdom. Its website includes information about many of the sites
    and legends associated with Robin Hood and his Merry Men (http://www.
    experiencenottinghamshire.com/robin-hood/robin-hood-legend/the-merry-men).

International Center of Medieval Art (ICMA)
The Cloisters
Fort Tryon Park
New York, NY 10040
(212) 928-1146
Website: http://www.medievalart.org
The ICMA supports research and education about medieval arts and sponsors studies,
    exhibitions, and publications committed to the art and culture of the Middle Ages.

The Medieval Institute
Western Michigan University
Kalamazoo, MI 49008-5432
(269) 387-8785
Website: http://wmich.edu/medieval
This institute encourages the study of medieval culture and literature and supports the
    publication of materials and research on the history of the Middle Ages.

The Metropolitan Museum of Art
1000 Fifth Avenue
New York, NY 10028-0198
(212) 535-7710
Website: http://www.met-museum.org
The Metropolitan Museum of Art has a world-renowned collection of artwork and
    artifacts and holds numerous special exhibitions annually. Its website includes
    information about the Crusades (1095–1291), including a slideshow of works
    of art and a timeline.

The National Gallery
The National Gallery Education
Trafalgar Square
London WC2N 5DN

United Kingdom

020 7747 2424

Website: http://www.nationalgallery.org.uk

This museum contains Daniel Maclise's painting *Robin Hood and His Merry Men Entertaining Richard the Lionheart in Sherwood Forest* (1839) and many other artworks of interest to people who enjoy studying the history of England and medieval literature.

The Sherwood Forest Trust

5&6 Church Farm Business Center

Mansfield Road

Edwinstowe

Nottinghamshire NG21 9NJ

United Kingdom

01623 821490

Website: http://sherwoodforest.org.uk

This organization supports the preservation and conservation of the region of Sherwood Forest and works to save its cultural heritage.

WEBSITES

Because of the changing nature of Internet links, Rosen Publishing has developed an online list of websites related to the subject of this book. This site is updated regularly. Please use this link to access the list:

http://www.rosenlinks.com/HERO/Robin

FOR FURTHER READING

Appleby, J. C., and Dalton, P., *Outlaws in Medieval and Early Modern England*, Ashgate, 2009

Baldwin, David, *Robin Hood: The English Outlaw Unmasked*, Amberley Publishing, 2011

Bradbury, J., *Robin Hood*, Amberley Publishing, 2010

Byrom, Jamie, and Riley, Michael, *The Crusades* (Enquiring History), Hodder Education, 2013

Cawthorne, Nigel, *A Brief History of Robin Hood*, Running Press Book Publishers, 2010

Child, F. J., *The English and Scottish Popular Ballads: vII*, Forgotten Books, 2007

Davies, Glyn, and Kennedy, Kirstin, *Medieval and Renaissance Art: People and Possessions*, Victoria & Albert Museum, 2009

Dixon-Kennedy, Mike, *The Robin Hood Handbook: The Outlaw in History, Myth and Legend*, The History Press, 2013

Green, Roger Lancelyn, *The Adventures of Robin Hood*, Puffin Books, 2010

Harasta, Jesse, and Rivers, Charles, editor, *Robin Hood: The History and Folklore of the English Legend*, Charles River Editors, 2013

Hattstein, Markus, and Udelhoven, Hermann-Josef, *Middle Ages and the Early Modern Period from the 5th Century to the 18th Century* (Witness to History: A Visual Chronicle of the World), Rosen Publishing, 2013

Holt, J. C., *Robin Hood*, Thames & Hudson, 1989

Knight, S., *Robin Hood: A Mythic Biography*, Cornell University Press, 2009

Matthews, R., *On the Trail of the Real Robin Hood*, Bretwalda Books, 2012

Mortimer, I., *The Time Traveller's Guide to Medieval England*, Vintage, 2009

Nolan, Scott Allen, *Robin Hood: A Cinematic History of the English Outlaw and His Scottish Counterparts*, McFarland & Company, Inc., 2008

Pollard, A. J., *Imagining Robin Hood*, Routledge, 2004

Prestwich, M., *Plantagenet England*, Oxford University Press, 2007

Pyle, Howard, *The Merry Adventures of Robin Hood and Other Stories*, Benedictine Classics, 2012

Rennison, Nick, *Robin Hood: Myth, History & Culture*, Oldcastle Books, Ltd., 2012

Schama, Simon, *A History of Britain: At the Edge of the World? 3500 BC–1603 AD*, Hyperion, 2000

INDEX